Comments on other *Amazing Stories* from readers & reviewers

"*Tightly written volumes filled with lots of wit and humour about famous and infamous Canadians.*"
Eric Shackleton, *The Globe and Mail*

"*The heightened sense of drama and intrigue, combined with a good dose of human interest is what sets* Amazing Stories *apart.*"
Pamela Klaffke, *Calgary Herald*

"*This is popular history as it should be... For this price, buy two and give one to a friend.*"
Terry Cook, a reader from Ottawa, on **Rebel Women**

"*Glasner creates the moment of the explosion itself in graphic detail...she builds detail upon gruesome detail to create a convincingly authentic picture.*"
Peggy McKinnon, *The Sunday Herald*, on **The Halifax Explosion**

"*It was wonderful...I found I could not put it down. I was sorry when it was completed.*"
Dorothy F. from Manitoba on **Marie-Anne Lagimodière**

"*Stories are rich in description, and bristle with a clever, stylish realness.*"
Mark Weber, *Central Alberta Advisor*, on **Ghost Town Stories II**

"*A compelling read. Bertin...has selected only the most intriguing tales, which she narrates with a wealth of detail.*"
Joyce Glasner, *New Brunswick Reader*, on **Strange Events**

"*The resulting book is one readers will want to share with all the women in their lives.*"
Lynn Martel, *Rocky Mountain Outlook*, on **Women Explorers**

CHRISTMAS IN ONTARIO

CHRISTMAS IN ONTARIO

Heartwarming Legends, Tales, and Traditions

HOLIDAY

by Cheryl MacDonald

PUBLISHED BY ALTITUDE PUBLISHING CANADA LTD.
1500 Railway Avenue, Canmore, Alberta T1W 1P6
www.altitudepublishing.com
1-800-957-6888

Extreme care has been taken to ensure that all information presented in
this book is accurate and up to date. Neither the author nor the
publisher can be held responsible for any errors.

Publisher	Stephen Hutchings
Associate Publisher	Kara Turner
Series Editor	Jill Foran
Editor	Gayl Veinotte

We acknowledge the financial support of the Government
of Canada through the Book Publishing Industry Development
Program (BPIDP) for our publishing activities.

Altitude GreenTree Program
Altitude Publishing will plant twice as many trees as were used
in the manufacturing of this product.

We acknowledge the support of the Canada Council for the Arts which
in 2003 invested $21.7 million in writing and publishing throughout Canada.

 Canada Council   Conseil des Arts
for the Arts   du Canada

National Library of Canada Cataloguing in Publication Data

MacDonald, Cheryl, 1952-
Christmas in Ontario / Cheryl MacDonald.

(Amazing stories)
Includes bibliographical references.
ISBN 1-55153-779-6

1. Christmas--Ontario. I. Title. II. Series: Amazing stories
(Canmore, Alta.)

GT4987.15.M33 2004   394.2663'09713   C2004-903753-6

An application for the trademark for Amazing Stories™
has been made and the registered trademark is pending.

Printed and bound in Canada by Friesens
2 4 6 8 9 7 5 3 1

For the Lewises
Rocky and Wilma,
Erica and Adam —

with warm memories of our
shared Christmas tradition

Contents

Prologue

Jimmy was a very sick boy. The rare lung ailment he had been suffering from for years kept him in the hospital at Christmastime. Doctors held little hope of recovery. His parents were struggling to pay his medical bills. Generous neighbours helped out occasionally by slipping five-dollar bills under the milk bottles on the front porch. Being in the hospital was so boring that sometimes he and the other young patients threw porridge at the ceiling just for something to do.

Christmas was the worst. The hours dragged on and on. He wanted to go home, wanted to be out of the hospital for good.

Then Santa arrived, and his spirits lifted. He was thrilled to see the familiar red suit and the flowing white beard. Santa's laughter made him feel better than any medicine could. As he looked around, he saw that other children felt the same way. It was absolutely wonderful the way so many sad little faces lighted up as the jolly old gentleman moved around the room.

All too soon, Santa was gone. After a few minutes, Jimmy wandered along the hospital corridor. Then he saw Santa — or was it? The man was sipping a glass of wine, and Jimmy suddenly realized this was a real person, not the magical bringer of Christmas presents. The white beard and hair were just a costume.

He also realized something else. If an ordinary man could play Santa Claus and bring joy to so many children, maybe he could, too. At that moment, Jimmy made a promise. If he ever got better, he would become Santa. He would visit children in hospitals, just as this Santa had done, and he would make them smile and forget about their problems for awhile.

Chapter 1
Christmas Traditions

I t happens every year. The days get shorter; the temperature drops. The sun seems to disappear for days on end as Ontarians brace themselves for winter, which, even in the moderate south, brings considerable snow and ice. But even as the darkness and chill settle in, there is a glimmer of hope, a feeling of growing excitement. For the start of winter also means the beginning of the Christmas season, a time of celebration that goes back to the earliest days of Ontario settlement and far beyond.

Christmas has been observed in Ontario since the mid-1600s, when French missionaries brought their religious and festive traditions with them to remote mission outposts. Later, when Europeans settled permanently in the province, they introduced other holiday customs, which eventually took root in the new land.

Over time, Christmas celebrations changed. Some were abandoned as old-fashioned or barbaric. New ones developed, although it can probably be argued that Ontario has no truly unique Christmas traditions. At some level, nearly every aspect of Christmas can be traced back hundreds of years, sometimes thousands, to winter solstice celebrations of the distant past. In that respect, Christmas in Ontario is fundamentally no different from Christmas in Quebec, or British Columbia, or, for that matter, Australia.

Yet, on another level, every Christmas is unique, as is every individual's experience of Christmas. It is a magical, mystical time, sometimes fraught with anxiety, pain, and longing, but more often full of hope and joy and goodwill towards all. How it is celebrated depends on the time and place and circumstances, but for most Ontarians Christmas has been, and probably will always be, one of the most memorable times of the year.

Ontario's First Christmas Carol
On Christmas Eve 1668, a 14-year-old girl lay fighting for her life at La Jeune Lorette, near Quebec City. Thérèse was a member of the Huron, a nation that had been pushed out of their traditional homelands near eastern Georgian Bay by the Iroquois. To comfort herself, as well as to mark the approaching holiday, she sang *Jesous Ahatonhia*, a carol

which described the birth of Christ in a setting that close-ly resembled the Ontario wilderness. Father Pierre-Joseph Chaumonot, the Jesuit who gave Thérèse the last rites, heard the song, which had been passed along among Christianized Hurons for many years. When Thérèse died on Christmas Day, he mentioned the song in passing. This was the first written reference to the "Huron Carol." Later transcribed and preserved for posterity, young Thérèse's favourite song was the first Canadian Christmas carol and probably the first carol written in North America.

While there is no definite proof, traditional accounts claim the carol was written by Father Jean de Brébeuf (1593–1649). A French missionary, Brébeuf was a skilled linguist who eventually wrote a Huron grammar and dictionary, so it is highly plausible that he translated the Christmas story into the Huron language. The words were set to the tune of an old French song, *La Jeune Pucelle* (The Young Maid).

Brébeuf first went to live among the Huron near Georgian Bay in 1626. In 1634, he was one of a group of Jesuit priests who revived a French mission at Sainte-Marie-Among-the-Hurons, near Midland. Located close to main canoe routes, Sainte Marie was designed to be a self-sup-porting European community, as well as a central mission for Christian Natives. For a time it flourished, and many of the Huron who visited learned the haunting song describing the birth of the Christ Child. But in 1648, the old enemies of the Huron, the Iroquois, began a series of attacks. The result was the martyrdom of several missionaries, including Brébeuf, who was killed on March 16, 1649. Two months later, the remaining missionaries abandoned Sainte Marie, burning what buildings remained.

Somehow, the song survived in the Huron language until it was written down by Father Étienne de Villeneuve. A Huron lawyer by the name of Paul Picard then translated it into French as *Jésus est né.* Finally, in 1926, poet Jesse Edgar Middleton provided English words:

'Twas in the moon of winter time
When all the birds had fled
That mighty Gitchi Manitou
Sent angel choirs instead
Before their light the stars grew dim
And wondering hunters heard the hymn:
"Jesus your King is born
Jesus is born: In excelsis gloria!"

Within a lodge of broken bark
The tender babe was found
A ragged robe of rabbit skin
Enwrapped his beauty 'round
And as the hunter braves drew nigh
The angel song rang loud and high:
"Jesus your King is born
Jesus is born: In excelsis gloria!"

The popularity of the song has grown tremendously since then, especially after Canada's centennial celebrations in 1967 awakened interest in Canadian history. *Jesous Ahatonhia*, the "Huron Carol," is now a Canadian Christmas tradition.

Pagan Roots

Although the "Huron Carol" was created specifically for Canada, it is part of a rich Christmas legacy stretching back to ancient times. While Christmas commemorates the birth of Jesus, many of our holiday customs are, in fact, pagan in origin. Since the sun was worshipped by most civilizations at one time or another, the winter solstice was an important date on most calendars. Starting in September, the sun's power gradually weakens until it reaches its lowest point in mid-December on the shortest day of the year. From then on, the days lengthen and the sun gains strength, a phenomenon that in ancient times was cause for celebration. So the Romans held Saturnalia, with gifts, revelry, and decorated homes.

As the Roman Empire and Christianity spread into Europe, other customs were blended with the traditions of Saturnalia, including those of the Germanic peoples in northern Europe and the Celtic Druids. Evergreens were highly prized as decorations — their ability to stay green while all other vegetation withered seemed magical. Ivy, used by the ancient Romans, was dedicated to the god Bacchus and was said to prevent drunkenness. Holly, also known in Roman times, was regarded by early Christians as the "holy tree." Some believed the wood had been used for Christ's cross, and the prickly leaves and red berries symbolized the crown of thorns. The Druids considered mistletoe a sacred plant, especially when it was found growing on oak trees, and harvested the leaves for use in ceremonies.

Although the mystical meanings of these plants were eventually forgotten, their presence remained essential at Christmastime, especially among homesick colonists.

Many early Ontario settlers were too busy with day-to-day survival to bother much with Christmas decorations. In 1828, describing workers on Ottawa's Rideau Canal, one anonymous pioneer wrote, "In Dow's great swamp, one of the most dismal places in the wilderness, did five Irishmen, two Englishmen, and one Scotchman hold their merry Christmas — or rather forgot to hold it at all." Some down-played Christmas celebrations because of religious reasons, a legacy from Puritan times when anything remotely resembling Catholic celebrations was banned. Yet others simply could not imagine Christmas without evergreens. Catharine Parr Traill was one of them.

Catharine was a genteel Englishwoman who, along with her husband and other relatives, including her sister, Susanna Moodie, immigrated to the Peterborough area in 1832. Catherine was 30 at the time, and Susanna was two years younger. Both wrote extensively of their experiences in the backwoods of Canada, including Catharine's nostalgia for the evergreens that decorated English homes and churches during the holidays. She and her husband had not yet settled into their own home, but that did not prevent her from wandering into the fields near the house where they were staying and gathering some wintergreen to hang on the mantel in their host's home. Although some laughed at her efforts, Catharine later wrote, "It seemed to me these green branches might be held as emblems to remind us that we should keep faith bright and green within our hearts."

By 1838, she was settled in her own house. In the previous 12 months, panic had swept through Upper Canada after rebellion broke out on December 5, 1837. The insurgents were quickly dispersed. Their leader, William Lyon Mackenzie, fled to the United States, but rumours of imminent violence put a damper on Christmas celebrations, as did the absence of many men on militia duty. Although rebels Samuel Lount and Peter Matthews were executed, and others were imprisoned or exiled to Australia, several additional attempts were made to overthrow the colonial government during 1838. In February, rebels attacked Pelee Island in western Lake Erie. In June, another force raided the Short Hills, south of St. Catharines. In November, rebels under Colonel Nils von Schoultz occupied a windmill and several houses near Prescott. The skirmishes that followed left 16 British-Canadian defenders dead and 60 wounded. A few weeks later, on December 4, Windsor was invaded.

Mrs. Catherine Parr Traill's house, "Westove,"
Lakefield, Ontario, August 1925.

Across Upper Canada, able-bodied men were called to
militia duty. Following the Prescott and Windsor raids, troops
were stationed in Toronto, the provincial capital. Among
them was Catharine's brother-in-law, John Moodie. Wanting
to distract her worried sister Susanna and Susanna's young
family, Catharine planned an English-style Christmas and
sent her hired man, Malachi, and a young servant, Martin, to
gather a sleigh-load of evergreens.

Christmas Traditions

The boughs and branches cheered up the Traills' log cabin considerably, but, Catharine wrote, "when all our green garlands were put up, we missed the bright-varnished holly and its gay, joy-inspiring red berries." Hannah, Catharine's English maid, remembered that wintergreen and cranberries grew in a nearby swamp and suggested them as a substitute. Unfortunately, the wintergreen was buried under a couple of feet of snow, so they had to make do with "the red transparent berries of the cranberry" and a string of coral beads belonging to Catharine's young daughter, Katie. These were woven among the hemlock boughs with satisfactory results.

Then Catharine sent an ox-drawn sleigh off to fetch Susanna and her family. Years later, she described the vehicle as humble and rude, but noted how pleasant a ride in one could be, especially through a snow-laden evergreen forest: "Reposing on a bed of hay, covered with buffalo or bear skins, or good wool coverlets, and wrapped in plaids, with well-wadded hoods, we were not a whit less happy than if we had been rolling along in a gay carriage, drawn by splendid horses."

Catharine's description of that pioneer Christmas was pblished in 1860 in *The Canadian Settler's Guide*, one of many books written in the nineteenth century to help prospective immigrants adjust to their new life in Canada. An earlier guidebook, this one by John Howison, described how one Christmas legend had crossed the ocean and been transplanted with a distinctively Canadian twist.

Christmas Critters

Animals have traditionally been associated with Christmas celebrations. Legend says that on the night when Christ was born, birds sang in the darkness and, above their song and the carolling of angels, the crowing of the cock could be heard, heralding the dawn of a new era. According to another tradition, the ox and the ass, omnipresent in Christmas cards and carols, warmed the Christ Child with their breath. Ever afterward, their descendants were given the gift of speech for a brief time on Christmas Eve. But they only spoke among themselves, and it was rumoured that anyone who attempted to eavesdrop might die trying. A related story claims that, recalling the adoration of the Christ Child on the first Christmas, animals kneel and bow to the east at midnight on Christmas Eve.

Animal folklore was probably the farthest thing from John Howison's mind one dark December night around 1820 when he went for a walk in the woods in southwestern Ontario. Above him were a bright moon and twinkling stars; around him were thousands of trees. The night was completely silent, except for the occasional rustle of the trees or the distant howl of a wolf. And then he saw something dark moving cautiously among the trees.

At first, Howison was convinced it was a bear, but as he moved slowly closer he discovered it was "an Indian on all fours." The Englishman hesitated, not quite sure what to make of this surprising individual and his peculiar position.

Then the other man waved his hand and put his finger to his lips, gesturing to Howison to be quiet.

"I approached him," Howison later wrote, " and, notwithstanding his injunction to silence, inquired what he did there. 'Me watch to see the deer kneel,' replied he; 'this is Christmas night, and all deer fall upon their knees to the Great Spirit, and look up.' The solemnity of the scene and the grandeur of the idea, alike contributed to fill me with awe. It was affecting to find traces of the Christian faith existing in such a place, even in the form of such a tradition."

Visions of Sugar Plum Fairies
While the origins of some Christmas traditions are lost in the mists of time, others have developed fairly recently. One example of this is *The Nutcracker*, the ballet which has become an integral part of Christmas celebrations in many North American cities. The ballet is based on "The Nutcracker and the King of Mice," a story written by E.T.A. Hoffman in 1812.The original story starts with a Christmas Eve party at the Stahlbaum house, during which the children, Clara and Fritz, are given two life-size dolls by their godfather, Drosselmeyer. Clara's gift is a beautiful nutcracker, which her brother deliberately breaks. Although Drosselmeyer fixes it, Clara is worried about the toy, and after everyone retires for the evening, she sneaks downstairs and falls asleep with the nutcracker in her arms. As she sleeps, she dreams that the toys under the tree, including the Nutcracker, come to life

and battle an army of mice. After defeating the King of Mice, the Nutcracker undergoes another transformation, this time becoming a prince who transports Clara to magical places, including the Land of Sweets, where they meet the Sugar Plum Fairy.

The story formed the basis for a ballet by Peter Tchaikovsky, which debuted in St. Petersburg, Russia, in 1892. Although Tchaikovsky was well known by this time, the ballet was never really popular in Russia or the rest of Europe. This changed after it crossed the Atlantic. By 1944, when *The Nutcracker* debuted in San Francisco, many audiences were familiar with the music, thanks to The Nutcracker Suite segment of Walt Disney's hit movie, *Fantasia.* The animated film, featuring dancing toadstools and magical frost fairies, made the music familiar to millions. After Russian choreographer George Balanchine mounted a lavish production in New York City in 1954, there was no looking back.

Jennifer Fisher, a dance historian and author of *Nutcracker Nation,* claims the ballet's appeal stems in part from family togetherness and communal celebration, and that it embodies "a spirit of Christmas everyone can share." The ballet is so popular that many dance companies rely on it as their major money-maker for the year. One of the most popular productions is that presented by the National Ballet School of Canada. On December 26, 1964, a version choreographed by National Ballet founder Celia Franca debuted at Toronto's O'Keefe Centre. *Toronto Daily Star* critic Nathan

Rehearsal of the National Ballet of Canada's 1968 production of the Tchaikovski-Ivanov ballet *The Nutcracker*. Toronto, Ontario, 1968.

Cohen commented at the time that the production needed work, especially in maintaining the illusion of "a world of frosty enchantment and glitter," but still seemed "likely to catch on immediately with the public."

It did, and the Franca production was performed for more than 20 years, until James Kudelka staged a new one in 1995, which has been performed by the National Ballet ever since. Aside from involving the entire company of the National Ballet, plus many children from the National Ballet School, *The Nutcracker* includes two roles for celebrity guests. The Cannon Dolls, who fire a cannon into the audience in Act I, have been played by such well-known Canadians as comedian Colin Mochrie, singer Murray McLaughlin, and newscaster Sandi Rinaldo. Meanwhile, other dance companies, both professional and amateur, have been staging *The Nutcracker* all across Ontario, making it one of the mainstays of the holiday season.

Lighting Up

Spectacle of some kind has always been part of Christmas, and lights are particularly important. Long ago, at the darkest season of the year, lighted candles created a kind of imitative magic, replacing the light of the waning sun. In Christian symbolism, lights were reminders of the Christ Child — the "Light of the World" — as well as the Star of Bethlehem, which pointed out his location to the Magi.

Today, almost every community in Ontario has some kind of decorative Christmas lights, which are often turned on with a formal light-up ceremony. London, Sarnia, Burlington, St. Thomas, and Owen Sound are among the many places that have established Christmas light festivals over the years. Probably the most spectacular, in terms of setting and sheer size, is the Niagara Falls Winter Festival of Lights. Billed as Canada's largest light festival, the event has been running since 1983. Concentrating on the falls, the Niagara River, and adjacent parkland, the award-winning two-month festival features more than 100 animated light displays and more than five kilometres of lights strung on trees. Many local homeowners and businesses also participate — at the Skylon Tower, some 5000 lightbulbs are arranged to turn the 160-metre (520-foot) structure into a giant Christmas tree. Set against the backdrop of the falls, with ice, snow, and mist adding extra sparkle, the Winter Festival of Lights has become one of Ontario's top Christmas attractions.

Because private businesses are also involved, no one is quite sure how many lights illuminate the festival, but estimates suggest there are close to a million. That is more than enough to dazzle the most jaded tourist. Yet, for many, one of the truly memorable features of the festival is the candlelight procession. Originally held in Queen Victoria Park, the event moved in 1997 to the outdoor Oakes Garden Theatre. Typically, around 2000 people turn out to light candles, walk through the park, sing carols, and watch a live nativity scene enacted by members of the Queensway Free Methodist Church. In the midst of blazing, state-of-the-art electrical displays, the candlelight and living tableau are poignant reminders of the origins of Christmas.

Compared to the Winter Festival of Lights, Simcoe's Panorama of Lights is a more modest event. But like the Niagara festival, it takes advantage of a lovely natural setting. And it claims to be the very first festival of lights in Ontario.

The light festival in this small town southeast of London began as a Santa Claus parade, an annual event meant to draw crowds to the town's downtown core and inspire them to start their Christmas shopping. By the late 1950s, there were concerns about the hazards of staging a single, short-run event so late in the year. One year, the temperatures were so frigid that the band's instruments froze. In 1957, the parade was delayed because of rain. The following year, cold, snowy weather threatened to keep the crowds away.

There was also some dissatisfaction about the amount of effort that went into preparing for an event that was over in a matter of minutes. Joan Daley, secretary of the Chamber of Commerce in the late 1950s, told writer Cheryl Bauslaugh, "We'd spend two weeks in the armouries building displays, and it was all over in about an hour."

Thinking that something more permanent might be the solution, organizers left two fairy tale floats in Wellington Park after the 1958 parade. There were immediate complaints from some residents who thought the Old Woman in the Shoe and Four-and-Twenty Blackbirds were ruining the town's charming riverside park. When the time to plan the next parade rolled around, the town's Retail Merchants' Association considered the possibility of establishing some kind of long-term Christmas attraction. Joan Daley and her husband Don presented a number of slides showing individual displays in other Ontario towns, including London and Dresden. There was some debate, but finally the association voted by a narrow margin to try a lighted display in Wellington Park.

From the outset, Joan was determined that Simcoe's festival of light would stand out. Although other communities had various lighted displays, Simcoe's would be different because the exhibits would be linked by themes, with similar themes located close together in the park. There were plans to recycle the best floats from the Santa Claus parade, but the group also decided to build three new displays. However, it was already October, so a lot of work had to be accomplished if the exhibits were going to be ready for Christmas.

Joan Daley took the lead by drafting a flyer to ask local businesses for financial support. Realizing she needed a name to make her pitch, she came up with Panorama of Christmas. Volunteers were recruited, and the group quickly raised nearly $2000. They also persuaded the town to pay for the cost of electricity needed to run the lights.

Right from the start, the exhibits focused on two main themes, faith and fantasy. For the first year, Panorama organizers moved four floats to the park: Santa and his reindeer, the Old Woman in the Shoe, Four-and-Twenty Blackbirds, and a giant poinsettia. To impart a religious element, three new exhibits were constructed: a giant open Bible telling the story of Christ's birth, a manger scene, and a church steeple.

In a few short weeks, three new exhibits were ready. To provide a touch of Christmas music, parks manager Grant Anderson, who lived next to Wellington Park, had a loudspeaker hooked up to his record player and persuaded his wife to keep the long-playing records going when the exhibit was lighted up.

The official opening was scheduled for November 27, 1959. As night fell, crowds of local residents, from babes-in-arms to senior citizens, gathered in the park. One by one, each of the exhibits lighted up. The very last was the church steeple, and just as the lights winked on, the strains of *Silent Night* floated into the darkness. "There wasn't a dry eye in the park," Joan Daley later recalled. "It was magical."

Since then, Simcoe's Panorama has drawn thousands of visitors each year. It has expanded from seven exhibits to more than 70, and is illuminated by more than 65,000 lights. It is not the biggest, nor the most ambitious light festival in Ontario, but the lighted scenes, surrounded by trees and reflected in the Lynn River, are right in the middle of the town's main thoroughfare, and anyone who travels through Simcoe on Highway 24 after dark is immediately drawn into the magic spell of Christmas light.

Chapter 2
Signs of the Season

Music is a part of most festivities, and Christmas is no exception. For centuries, special songs have been associated with the holidays. Frequently, the songs were sung by groups of revellers who travelled from house to house, both to bring Christmas cheer to the inhabitants and to collect treats or gifts for themselves or others.

When Georgina and Frederick Hyde celebrated their Christmas at Port Maitland in 1841, the evening ended with Georgina pulling her harp from the corner of the parlour and the family singing carols. Whether pioneer settlers had the inclination to go carolling door to door probably depended on the time, how well established a community was, and the fashion. Carolling apparently went in and out of fashion, as a writer for the *Niagara Mail* suggested in 1853: "For our part, we should be glad to see the revival of carol-singing that is, in a properly decorous spirit. There is something solemn and touching even now in listening to the chant of the street minstrels ... as it rises through the silence of the night, making one feel that peace and goodwill may become something more than sound."

Among the songs the anonymous writer may have heard were "The First Nowell" (the archaic spelling of Noel) and "God Rest Ye Merry Gentlemen," which had been brought to Canada by British immigrants in the early years of settlement. As the years passed, other carols arrived. In time, many became so well known that they were parodied. One parody with an Ontario connection is the "Twelve Days of Christmas" as sung by the McKenzie brothers, a.k.a. Rick Moranis and Dave Thomas. Moranis, who was born in Toronto, and Thomas, originally from St. Catharines, were well known for their portrayal of two "stupid hosers." In 1981, the brothers recorded an album of humorous songs, including their version of the traditional Christmas carol, in which the usual gifts from their true love were replaced with beer, two turtlenecks, three French toasts, four pounds of back bacon, five golden tuques and other odd items.

While a dash of humour or a modern version of a carol can be welcome, most Ontarians prefer to hear and sing well-loved traditional carols at Christmastime. And sometimes, the music can be put to work for a good cause. In 1924, hundreds of residents of Windsor designated Christmas Eve as the night to make music and raise money for charity. As members of the Border Cities Carolers society, they were divided into various teams, each with its own captain, who set out the areas they were to cover. Windsor residents had been told in advance that the carollers would be collecting for various charities and were reminded to give generously. In addition, just prior to Christmas Eve, society president J.R. Hewer requested that all city clergymen ask members of their congregations to think about opening their homes to the carollers, especially if the weather was extra cold. Meanwhile, various restaurants in the town offered free lunches to the singers.

The singing started at 6 p.m., with about 800 people participating. A local newspaper commented enthusiastically on how quickly the membership had increased in just a few short years. "The Border Cities Carolers have grown to a truly great organization composed of self-sacrificing men and women who will spend Christmas Eve bringing joy to the hearts of Border Cities' residents, with their Yuletide songs of cheer."

Over the years, other Ontario communities have made Christmas music in other ways. In 2001, more than 200 people poured into St. Mary's Church in Fort Frances on the Sunday before Christmas to hear *Hope was Born*, the story of the birth of Jesus. Music and narration was provided by the Choraliers, a 72-member community choir. The cantata, part of a Fort Frances Christmas tradition dating back to 1990, thrilled both listeners and participants, who agreed the music was just perfect for putting people in the Christmas spirit.

In 2002, the cathedral choir of St. Paul's Church in London, Ontario, travelled to St. Paul's Cathedral in London, England, to replace the English choir for a few days. Among the songs the 34-member choir performed was the *Huron Carol.* Although it added a distinctivly Canadian touch to the performance, it was especially appropriate for the cathedral — like the carol, St. Paul's dates from the 17th century.

While listening to carollers or choirs perform can be very enjoyable, for many people much of the fun in Christmas music is in singing along. Certainly this was the case one morning in 1945 when Christmas shopping came to a standstill for 20 minutes in the Toronto Simpson's store. As the 200-member staff choir lined up on the escalator and sang to the accompaniment of the Harmony Brass Quartet and the 48th Highlanders regimental band, customers, including harried mothers with young children, joined in. The choir had been conducted by 82-year-old A.P. Howells since 1921, and by this time its ability to soothe pre-Christmas nerves was legendary. According to the *Toronto Daily Star,* in the early 1940s one of the choir's brief concerts was broadcast over the radio. In New York, a harried cab company manager was struggling to find transportation for time-pressed customers. Partly to drown out their demands, he turned up the volume on his radio as the Simpson choir was singing. In a few minutes, the angry demands stopped. Everyone was too busy singing along to worry about getting a taxi, and for several years after that customers made a point of coming to the cab company for the week before Christmas just for the fun of singing Christmas carols.

Birds and Bells

In olden days, hand-bell ringers often accompanied carollers. The association of bells with Christmas, like so many other traditions, dates back to ancient times. Noisemaking was once thought to drive off evil spirits, but is now simply part of the general merriment. Hand-bells are most frequently used by volunteers collecting for charity, often dressed in Santa costumes or in Salvation Army uniforms. The familiar jingle of sleigh bells is one clue that Santa is on his way. Church bells ring out on Christmas Eve and Christmas Day, calling the faithful to worship and proclaiming the birth of the Christ child.

Unlike carols and bells, some seasonal traditions are best abandoned. One of the most barbaric has to do with birds. Today, the two birds most closely associated with Christmas are the dove, which symbolizes peace on earth, and the famous partridge in the pear tree. But centuries ago, Yuletide celebrations also included a wren. At one time, it was thought to be the "king of birds," and it was considered very bad luck to harm a wren — except on December 26.

Although best known to us as Boxing Day, the day after Christmas is also the Feast of St. Stephen. According to Christian tradition, Stephen was the first saint martyred after the crucifixion. Because he was stoned to death, his feast day was at one time celebrated by stoning a wren. Scholars speculate that the tradition may have been derived from pagan rituals involving the killing of a divine animal in order to claim some of its power. In some places, the wren hunt ended with the bird being carried from house to house and the hunters asking for treats. Those who provided drinks or other goodies were given a feather from the bird as a token of thanks and a good luck charm.

Over the years, the tradition was modified. By the time it reached Ontario, it had developed into a Boxing Day hunt in which various birds, squirrels, and other small animals were killed. Through much of the 19th century, a significant number of Ontarians sensed no irony in hunting or shooting during the season of peace. During the afternoon of Christmas Day, 1865, a "pleasant and interesting" shooting match took place at Twelve Mile Creek (St. Catharines). Meanwhile, Uncle Tom's Cabin, a Toronto tavern, was the scene of cockfights attended by 40 or 50 men. "Cursing and swearing and rowdyism" characterized the event, according to a contemporary newspaper report. "The birds were matched in this wicked sport - some seven rounds were fought - money changed hands - there were hard, angry protestations - and, at the last, a general fight, in which wounds and bruises were freely exchanged."

By this time, cockfighting was already considered less than respectable. Hunting and shooting, however, continued for many years, sometimes in the form of a turkey shoot. In 1893, a turkey shoot was staged at McDowall's Grounds, Toronto, on Christmas Day. Marksmen competed for prizes by shooting artificial birds and live sparrows. Then, for Christmas 1900, American ornithologist Frank Chapman made a suggestion that eventually replaced holiday hunting with an environmentally friendlier alternative. He asked bird-watching groups across North America to go out and count birds in their immediate area on Christmas Day. Twenty-seven conservationists were involved in that first count. Today, thousands are involved worldwide. In Ontario, bird-watching groups in more than 100 communities participate. In such diverse locations as Amherst Island, Wawa, Caledon, and Vankleek Hill, participants typically get up at the crack of dawn one morning between December 14 and January 5. They then cover a 24-kilometre circle, noting every bird they encounter. The information they gather is important in tracking population levels and distribution of birds. In 2002, for instance, worries about West Nile virus had birders paying closer attention to the species most heavily affected, including bluejays, but counters in the Fort Frances area discovered the number of jays was about the same as usual.

Christmas Weather

Although many Ontarians may not realize it, dreaming of a white Christmas has as much to do with folk beliefs about health and luck as it does with picture-perfect holiday scenery. British and European folklore suggest that a green Christmas is a bad omen, as a St. Catharines newspaper reminded readers in 1865: "If the old saw be true that 'A green Christmas makes a fat churchyard,' then will the undertakers and grave-diggers of this section of Canada be the most prosperous and happy individuals found hereabouts next spring and summer, for the snow is all or nearly gone — and there was very little of it to go — and the weather is as mild and as entertaining as a young miss of sixteen with her first beau."

While it is fairly unusual, Christmas has occasionally coincided with unseasonably warm temperatures in Ontario. In 1893, Lady Aberdeen, wife of Canada's governor-general, described her first Christmas in Canada as a "horrible muggy day." Although the weather had been chilly earlier in the month, just before Christmas the temperature had suddenly soared. There were some very disappointed youngsters in the Aberdeen household. "Great lamentations over no skating or snow sports for to-day," Lady Aberdeen wrote. To make matters worse, it started to rain when the family was out visiting. "It was ridiculous to see the rain freezing as it fell & making it quite difficult to shut one's umbrella."

In 1923, Christmas in the Bay of Quinte area was so warm that many residents went for a sail on Lake Ontario.

Meanwhile, in Stratford, F. Crocker found strawberries ready for picking in his garden. The following year, the *London Free Press* reported roses and primroses blooming a few days before Christmas. In 1994, when the temperature in Sault Ste. Marie climbed to eight degrees Celsius on Christmas Day, people put on bathing suits, sat outdoors on lawn chairs, or washed their cars.

Warm Christmas temperatures might be welcome as a respite from an Ontario winter, but they can also create additional hazards. In 1973, warmer temperatures in southern Ontario created serious, prolonged fog over several days, stranding thousands of holiday travellers. Six years later, five days of heavy rain dumped 100 millimetres of water on Toronto just before Christmas. Rivers rose to record heights, storm sewers overflowed and basements flooded — but at least no one had to shovel the water. If the temperature had been a bit lower, it was estimated, the rain would have been transformed into 100 centimetres of snow, about the equivalent of a typical year's snowfall.

Despite the occasional December heat waves, most Ontarians do get their share of white Christmases. Catharine Parr Traill described a fairly typical one in the Peterborough area in the 1830s and how much her children enjoyed it: "A merry day it was to them, for our boy Martin had made them a little sledge, and there was a famous snowdrift against the garden fence, which was hard packed and frozen smooth and glare. Up and down this frozen heap did James and Kate with their playmates glide and roll. It was a Christmas treat to watch those joyous faces, buoyant with mirth, and brightened by the keen air, through the frosty panes; and often was the graver converse of the parents interrupted by the merry shout and gleesome voices of their little ones; and if a sadder train of thought brought back the memory of former days, and home, country, and friends, from whom we were for ever parted, such sadness was not without its benefit, linking us in spirit to that home, and all that made it precious to our hearts."

The day was so enjoyable that when it was over, Catharine was reluctant to part with her sister Susanna, and so she accompanied her to her home. They weren't the only revellers on the road: "Just as we were issuing forth for our moonlight drive through the woods, our ears were saluted by a merry peal of sleigh bells, and a loud hurrah greeted our homely turn-out, as a party of lively boys and girls, crammed into a smart painted cutter, rushed past at full speed. They were returning from a Christmas merry-making at a neighbour's house, where they too had been enjoying a happy Christmas, and long the still woods echoed with the gay tones of their voices, and the clear jingle of their merry bells, as a bend in the river-road, brought them back on the night breeze to our ears."

While cold weather and snow could bring Christmas fun, sometimes it caused problems on Christmas Day. In 1872, the Marchioness of Dufferin and Ava was in Ottawa with her husband, the governor-general. Christmas morning was extremely chilly, with temperatures reading 28 degrees Celsius below zero. "Proprieties out of the question," Lady Dufferin wrote in her diary, then continued, "Must go to church in sealskin turbans, and must undress when we get there, as we sit near the stove; so that when we leave, the amount of things to be put on is frightful. There are my cloak, and my cloud, [a long scarf, wound several times around the neck] fur gauntlets, and woolen cuffs."

There were also several children to dress, including her son Fred, who was extremely nervous about the possibility of freezing his ears. "He is always feeling them and inquiring from passers-by whether they are frozen," she wrote. Fortunately for the Dufferins, just about everyone in church was busy putting on their own outer garments, so any commotion they made was lost in the general rush to get dressed and hurry home for Christmas celebrations. And given the heat in the building, Fred apparently did not have to worry about the state of his ears.

Christmas Amusements
From about the middle of the 1800s, school concerts and festivals were an important part of holiday festivities. In 1862, the *St. Catharines Journal* described a Sunday school festival for children of the St. James Church congregation, Port Dalhousie. It was held on Christmas Eve at the village schoolhouse. About 60 children attended, along with their

parents, other relatives, and friends, so the one-room school was packed to overflowing. The children sat in the front seats, close enough to get a good look at a Christmas tree that had been decorated specially for them. "Brilliantly lit up," the tree held "a splendid crop of all sorts of juvenile attractions" including books, dolls, trumpets, baskets, and other items.

In small rural communities, the school Christmas concert was one of the social highlights of the year. In fact, many teachers' reputations and continued employment depended on how good their Christmas concert was. In *I Remember the One-Room School*, a Guelph area teacher, Myrtle Fair, tells the story of one school inspector who felt a teacher should be fired because her pupils were so far behind with their work. The school trustees, however, insisted on keeping her because she staged the best Christmas concerts.

Staging a good Christmas concert took a lot of hard work. Typically, there were weeks of rehearsals and preparation, sometimes including time spent placating parents who felt their sons or daughters deserved a better part in the presentation. Despite all the planning, when the big night arrived, there was usually a problem or two. Students forgot their lines or fell off the low platform at the front of the classroom that usually served as a stage. Most of the time, teachers were able to take these minor mishaps in stride, which occasionally even provided a bit of amusement. One rural Ontario teacher told how Santa arrived by sleigh for a 1938 Christmas concert. Everyone inside the school heard the jingle of bells, but when several minutes passed and Santa had still not entered the classroom, someone was sent out to check on him. A short time later, Santa made his appearance. His cap was crooked and it was apparent to most adults in the room that he was "high as a kite." He had obviously swallowed a little too much Christmas cheer, but was still very amusing as he spoke to the group and handed out gifts to the children. Nevertheless, the teacher was extremely relieved when Santa — actually a member of the school board — got back into his sleigh and drove away.

Another teacher recalled asking her brother to play Santa for her school concert. When he reached the schoolhouse, he found the front entrance so jammed with spectators that he couldn't get in. Instead, he grabbed a ladder, took it around to the side of the schoolhouse, and climbed in the window. The unorthodox entrance got plenty of attention, but nothing compared to the polka that Santa insisted on dancing with the teacher. While the pianist played mightily, Santa and the teacher danced around the platform at the front of the classroom. But the mask Santa was wearing kept slipping, blocking his vision. At one point, he danced the teacher right off the platform and the young woman found herself dangling in mid-air. Fortunately, Santa kept his grip, pulled her back to safety, and the crowd cheered.

The Big Day Arrives
After weeks of anticipation, once presents are opened and

dinner is eaten, Christmas can sometimes deteriorate into boredom. Congenial company can alleviate that, especially if everyone can be involved in some sort of pleasant activity. In 1855, when the Royal Canadian Rifles were stationed at Kingston, they solved the problem of what to do on Christmas Day by strapping on skates, rounding up a lacrosse ball and some field hockey sticks, and playing on the ice of Lake Ontario. In so doing, they played what may have been the first hockey game recorded in Canada.

Board games and parlour games are another way to pass the time. In some cultures, Christmas Eve has also been recognized as a good time to practice a little fortune telling. Historian W.S. Wintemberg reported that young German-Canadian women in the Kitchener area had a way of finding out something about their future husbands on Christmas Eve in the late 19th and early 20th centuries. First, a cup was part-ly filled with water. Around midnight, being careful to keep completely silent, the girl poured a small amount of melted lead into the water. As it cooled, she looked at the shape, which was supposed to tell her the occupation of her future husband. A horseshoe suggested a blacksmith, while a square block might have indicated a farmer. Other Ontario amuse-ments over the years included skating outdoors, sleighing, or attending special Christmas concerts.

In 1935, one of the ways Ontarians could pass Christmas was in talking about the Dionne quintuplets of Callander. The media darlings were 19-month-old, dark-haired, mischievous toddlers who had just learned to turn on the lights in their nursery. A Christmas tree had been brought into the hospital where Dr. Allan Dafoe looked after them, and by Christmas Eve, plenty of pictures had already been taken by reporters. There were plans to have the quints' parents join them for Christmas dinner, along with their other siblings. Meanwhile, some quadruplets in New Brunswick would be enjoying a good Christmas dinner thanks to the quintuplets' guardians. On December 20, Canadian Press reported that the Mahaney quadruplets — the only quadruplets in Canada at the time — were facing a bleak Christmas. It was the middle of the Depression and the family, which included three other children, had fallen behind on their rent. Unless William Mahaney and his wife could come up with the $24 owing by December 23, the family would be forced to sell their household effects and move.

When they heard the news, the quints' guardians, Ontario minister of welfare David Croll, Dr. Dafoe, and Judge J.A. Valin, wired some cash to the Mahaneys. The amount was not disclosed, but it was "sufficient to cover arrears in rent." In effect, the three men had sent Christmas wishes from Ontario to New Brunswick, enclosing a little something extra.

Season's Greetings
Transmitting Christmas holiday wishes across great distances probably started as soon as people began writing letters,

but it wasn't until 1839 that the first Christmas cards were invented. Sir Henry Cole, who worked for the British Postal Service, hired an artist to create three Christmas scenes on a single piece of paper. On the left was a depiction of the hungry being fed, on the right was a scene of the needy being clothed. In the centre was a happy family sitting around the dinner table. The card also bore the familiar greeting "A Merry Christmas and A Happy New Year to You." From that beginning, the Christmas card gradually evolved.

By 1875, the first Christmas cards were being printed in the United States. By 1884, a Kingston, Ontario newspaper, the *Daily British Whig*, could describe the practice of exchanging cards as a "pretty custom" that was "largely on the increase." The newspaper went on to provide details of the cards that were available in local stores that year. Prices ranged from a few cents to $10, depending on the quality and the material from which they were made. Some were quite elaborate fabrications, shaped like crosses or books and covered in plush. Others were miniature works of art. The writer of the article was particularly impressed by cards with floral themes, noting they were "a very good imitation of hand-painting and in designs of full-blown thistle blossoms, golden rod and clover heads." Inscriptions on the various cards included "Health, wealth and love of many friends" or "May peace be thine and joy within thy heart."

Over the next hundred years or so, Christmas cards evolved to include cartoon characters, humorous messages,

A Christmas card from 1907.

and sometimes lights and music. They have become an easy and relatively inexpensive way to send greetings. Even though thousands of identical cards may be purchased and sent, the messages they bear are usually carefully selected by the sender and much appreciated by the receiver. But the Christmas cards that seem to be most touching are the greetings sent to Canadian military personnel and peacekeepers at Christmastime.

In 2001, a young woman from Johnstown, Ontario, spearheaded a national campaign to send cards overseas to military personnel stationed in Afghanistan, in the Middle

East, Bosnia, Germany, Belgium, and England. Chantel Christensen's effort started out small, with cards coming in from surrounding Leeds and Grenville counties. Many were sent by schoolchildren, some of them with personal notes or drawings. Eventually, cards started coming in from all across the country. One church in Prince Edward Island sent 731 cards to Chantel's "Let Them Know We Care" campaign. In all, well over 4000 cards were gathered. Just before they were loaded onto a transport truck for shipment to Ottawa, Reverend Arlyce Schiebout of Johnstown United Church blessed them. The minister also blessed the people who had sent the cards, speaking of the generosity of spirit that had motivated them to think of others.

The cards and messages of love and encouragement touched the hearts of many soldiers serving far from home. One of them was Master Warrant Officer Claude Bolduc. While his wife and three children were at home in Trenton, he was flying on a mission in the Persian Gulf. It was just another working day, no special holiday activities, no festive dinner. But what set it apart was a small package, from a small Ontario town, filled with Christmas greetings. As he later told a reporter, "You say, 'yes, it's Christmas after all'."

Chapter 3
Christmas Trees, Christmas Treats

For most of us, one of the most important symbols of Christmas is the tree. The custom of decorating trees goes back to pagan times, when ribbons and coloured objects were hung on them as offerings to the tree spirits. One Scandinavian legend tells how two lovers were killed by brigands in the forest. A fir tree grew out of the bloody soil and flaming lights were seen on it every year. Gradually, families in the area adopted the custom of decorating fir trees in their own homes with candles, a practice which eventually spread to other parts of Scandinavia.

The tradition of the tree is also linked to the Yule log, a ritual celebrated in Britain as far back as medieval times. On Christmas Eve, a large tree was cut down and its branches lopped off. Then it was dragged inside and thrown on the fire, where it was supposed to burn for the 12 days of Christmas. The tradition was still observed when the first permanent settlers reached Ontario. According to Lillian Gray, in 1783 a Reverend Mr. Stuart travelled from Kingston to a log cabin near Maitland to perform a marriage on Christmas Day. "The bare little log house was gay with spruce boughs and sprays of red rowan berries, and the ceremony took place where the dancing light from the Yule log lighted the faces of the bride and groom." The "rowan" berries were actually those of the mountain ash, which other settlers also used as a substitute for bright red holly berries. In 1855, for instance, Grimsby's Anglican church was decorated with evergreens and mountain ash berries.

At this point, Christmas trees were just beginning to become popular in Ontario.

Germany is considered the home of the modern Christmas tree, although stories about the tree stretch back to the time of St. Boniface, the missionary who Christianized parts of Germany around the eighth century. The English saint was determined to eliminate pagan customs from the country. In one town, after he cut down the sacred oak tree, he placated furious citizens by offering them a fir tree as a symbol of the new faith. Martin Luther, himself the founder of a new faith, is also said to have originated the decorated tree. Overcome by the glory of the stars in the winter sky one evening, he rushed home, trying to express his feelings to his family. Unable to do so in words, he chopped a tree from the garden, set it in the nursery, and lighted candles amid the dark boughs.

The German custom of decorated Christmas trees was introduced to the English world in the 1840s, shortly after Queen Victoria married Prince Albert. The new royal consort was German and brought with him the custom of decorating a tree. But parts of Canada were already familiar with the custom by then. In 1781, General Friedrich von Riedesel and his wife introduced the Christmas tree at Sorel, Quebec. Meanwhile, immigrants of German extraction, including Mennonites and others who fled to Upper Canada following the American Revolution, brought their Christmas tree traditions with them. Until the mid-Victorian period, almost the only place in Ontario where a Christmas tree could be found was in a Mennonite or German home. The first trees were usually small enough to fit on a table, but by the late 1800s, sturdy metal stands made it possible to bring enormous trees into the house.

Early decorations were usually handmade, or items found around the house. Straw ornaments or strings of cranberries were popular, as well as candles. Paper and bits of cloth were also used, sometimes shaped into decorative items. By the 1870s, commercial decorations were widely available. Most were imported from Germany and could be purchased at any sizeable store.

One superstition claims that a well-decorated tree

ensures good fortune for a household during the coming year. There are also certain superstitions surrounding other Christmas greenery. To avoid family quarrels, holly should not be brought into the house until Christmas Eve. It's unlucky to crush the berries underfoot or to carry a flowering plant indoors. For good luck, the first person to enter a house in the new year should carry a holly sprig, and, once the holidays are over, the plant should be burned.

Kissing under the mistletoe is also said to bring good luck in the coming year. The practice dates back to at least the 17th century, and, although the rules relaxed over the years, there were once certain standard practices. According to tradition, a girl may not refuse to be kissed under the mistletoe, but the man must play fair and pluck a berry as he kisses the lady of his choice. When the berries are gone, the kissing stops.

Of course, a woman who wanted to attract the attention of a particular man could make sure she was "caught" under the mistletoe. Another English custom dictated that any single man who refused to kiss a girl under the mistletoe had to give her a pair of gloves. However, not all immigrants were familiar with the mistletoe custom and first encountered it in Ontario. In her diary, Mary Hallen, who lived in the Penetanguishene area, described an 1852 Christmas gathering where hemlock was hung in a drawing room as a substitute for mistletoe. When two of the young men present seemed reluctant to kiss a certain Miss Hodgett, the lady took matters into her own hands by kissing the gentlemen herself. "How strange," Mary commented in her diary. "It is not English I am sure not Canadian, perhaps it is a wild Irish custom." One of the young men Miss Hodgett kissed was Mary's brother Edgar, who was teased so much by another brother, Preston, at breakfast the following morning that it caused his face "to resemble the rising sun on an Indian summer morning."

Whether or not Ontarians subscribed to the superstitions and practices surrounding Christmas greenery, one thing is for certain: trends in decorating change over time. In the 1920s, theme trees were popular. During the war years, patriotic items, such as small Union Jacks, sometimes adorned Christmas trees. In the 1960s, artificial trees became wildly popular. Some were made of material that resembled toilet brushes dyed green, or, for the more adventurous, pink or white. Aluminium trees were the rage for a time, too. People loved the convenience of an artificial tree — you only had to shop for it once, and there was no need to pick pine needles out of the carpet from December through April. And those who still wanted the lovely fragrance of a real evergreen without all the fuss could buy spray-on scent.

The choice of a Christmas tree and its decorations depended largely on personal taste. Some people simply followed their own fancy, but others looked to experts for advice. In 1966, avant-garde Toronto artist Harold Town discussed his preferences in *Maclean's Magazine*. First of all, he recommended that the Christmas tree be spruce. "Scotch pine is not a Christmas tree, it is an inverted toilet brush." Most of his suggestions for decorating the tree were common sense: start from the top and work down, using the smaller decorations nearer the top and the larger ones at the bottom. He was definitely against handmade ornaments, even those made by children. But he did encourage readers to involve their children in decorating the tree, although he suggested the younger ones handle unbreakable ornaments, which he suggested should be hung deep inside the tree near the bottom.

Choosing the Perfect Tree
Harold Town did not discuss the business of selecting a tree, but it was something most Ontarians knew about from personal experience. As late as the 1960s, in rural areas especially, some people were still cutting their trees in local forests, just as their ancestors had done for generations.

There was relatively little risk involved in harvesting a tree from the wild, although in one case the hunt for a Christmas tree inadvertently led to tragedy. Ernie Elvish was seven-and-a-half and living in Fort William (Thunder Bay). On Monday, December 15, 1924 he went out with a friend, Jackie Saunders, to find Christmas trees for their homes. During their search, the boys argued about the right way home and parted company.

Snow was already falling when the boys separated. A

few hours later, Ernie's parents reported him missing. As the temperature plummeted to several degrees below zero, a search party was organized. Jackie, who had made it home safely, led the searchers to the last place he had seen Ernie. Although the snow had covered their footprints, searchers doggedly combed the bush, looking for traces of the missing boy.

The snowfall and the frigid cold soon dashed hopes that the boy would be found alive. Still, the searches continued with city employees, police officers, and private citizens joining in. Walking six feet apart, every man probed the ground in front of him with a staff in an attempt to find some trace of Ernie. Although some believed there was little hope of finding anything before spring, the search continued through Wednesday and Thursday, fanning out five kilometres from where Ernie was last seen.

On Friday morning, the postman delivered a package from a Winnipeg store. Inside were boots and skates that Mrs. Elvish had ordered for her son's Christmas. When she saw them, she broke down. "Bring me back my son," she told searchers. "Get his body even though he is dead. I cannot stand the thought of him lying in the snow." That afternoon, three Finnish volunteers with the search party spied a dark area in the snow. On closer inspection, they found Ernie's body, partly covered by a snowdrift. He had apparently walked more than two kilometres by himself in the storm before collapsing.

Despite Jackie's safe return, Ernie's death was a tragic ending to what should have been a happy holiday outing. Fortunately, for most people, choosing a tree was a pleasant experience, one that was often filled with nostalgia. Writing in the *Sault Ste. Marie Star* in 1929, Isabel Peycott ruminated on how much town residents owed country folks for their Christmas cheer. She described a scene at the local market on a Saturday in mid-December when Joseph Roberts of Korah brought in a sled filled with balsam and spruce. "Even people who had no idea of buying one just then, gathered around the sleigh and there was an understanding smile around that meant such a lot, as if they were thinking, 'Remember how we used to go out and get one like this and haul it in, and put it in place'." Various comments passed as the people made their selections. Some of the "old boys" talked about how they liked cedar at Christmas, while "an old girl" preferred spruce and another woman insisted balsam was essential "to make the right Christmas fragrance."

In more recent years, Christmas tree farms have become increasingly popular. Today, almost all trees sold in the province come from farms. Only about 10 percent of a tree farmer's crop is harvested in any one year. The rest remains in the field, waiting for another holiday season. Many of these farms are family-run operations where customers can pick out their own tree before it is cut. Like other kinds of farming, it is a business operation, but that doesn't mean the owners lack Christmas spirit. In 2003, the Victorian Country

Christmas Tree Farm in Scugog donated $5 from every tree to Habitat for Humanity of North Durham.

Christmas trees have been turned into fundraisers in other ways, too. Since 2000, Sharbot Lake has held an annual festival of trees sponsored by the Villages Beautiful Committee, which looks after all the communities in Central Frontenac county. Participants, both individuals and organizations, buy trees in three different sizes — four feet, six feet, and eight feet — then decorate them at their own expense, usually following a theme of some kind, such as teddy bears or candies. Once the trees are decorated, the public is invited to view them at a local community hall. They are also able to buy tickets for a chance to win their favourite tree. After three days, the winning names are drawn. The event raises money for community causes and also brings in donations for the area food bank.

Food and Feasting

While Christmas trees provide a feast for the eyes, the holiday simply is not complete without a real feast as well. A few centuries back, the English celebrated with a boar's head. To Christians, the animal symbolized Satan and its slaughter recalled Christ's triumph over evil. Apparently, the English custom was a Christianized version of a Germanic folk tale, for it was said that the god Freyr rode his boar Gullinbusti, and during Freyr's festival of Yuletide, a boar was slain in his honour. About the only trace of the legend to reach Canada was a song celebrating the event, "The Boar's Head Carol," which is seldom heard today.

They may have preferred to leave the tradition of the boar's head behind them, but Ontario's early settlers still went all out to pack the table with holiday goodies. Many women spent weeks preparing for the holiday, hoarding various dried fruits, sugar, and other items to make into plum pudding, fruitcake, and mincemeat tarts. One early Niagara Peninsula settler, finding he had no raisins or spices, added several cakes of maple sugar to his pudding. It turned out just fine.

Plum pudding was often made on the last Sunday before Advent in order to give it time to ripen, and was one of the most popular Christmas dishes through much of the 19th century. Even the prisoners at Kingston Penitentiary received a share — in 1886, a half-ton of pudding was prepared for their Christmas dinner.

In 1837, Catharine Parr Traill's Christmas dinner consisted of "A glorious goose, fattened on the rice-bed in our lake." Years later she noted that, in this period, "turkeys were only to be met with on old cleared farms in those days, and beef was rarely seen in the back-woods." Yet, when the extended family of Georgina and Frederick Hyde of Port Maitland sat down to their Christmas dinner in 1841, their sumptuous menu included a number of wild turkeys, which are considerably smaller than the modern domestic variety. The Hydes also enjoyed home-cured ham, applesauce made from their own orchard, and plum pudding that had been liberally doused with brandy and set afire

Talking Turkey

Turkeys, which are native to the Americas, had been known in Europe for a couple of hundred years at this point. Although some Ontarians preferred the British tradition of serving a Christmas goose, turkeys were featured on many menus, and by the late 1800s were considered absolutely essential to most Christmas dinners. In 1897, the *Globe* reported that a wide selection was available at the Toronto market. That holiday season, turkey was selling for between eight and nine cents a pound, and among the birds was a huge gobbler that tipped the scale at 43 pounds. In 1898, the *New Galt Cookbook* recommended turkey as the centrepiece of a lavish Christmas menu that included oyster soup, cranberry sauce, and mashed potatoes. A similar menu, this one from a 1901 issue of the *Perth Courier*, suggested oysters on the half shell, consommé, fish, browned potatoes, turkey, and cranberry moulds, along with various vegetables, pickles, and sweets.

Turkey had become so much a part of Ontarians' Christmas celebrations that some businesses used them as promotional items. In the late 1880s and early 1890s, P. Jamieson, owner of the Palace Clothing House at Toronto's Yonge and Queen Streets, offered "a beautiful, well-fed, live Turkey" to any customer who bought at least $7.50 worth of goods. Companies gave birds to their employees as Christmas bonuses. In 1900, the Toronto Railway Company distributed a total of five tons of turkeys to its employees. Many charitable organizations also tried to ensure that poor families received a turkey in their Christmas baskets.

For those unable to obtain a bird, there was always the option of stealing one. In 1897, William Boylan of Hamilton stole a turkey from a sleigh owned by Robert Hannah. The boy was arrested and sent to Mimico Industrial School for three years. The following year, a wandering Willowdale turkey resulted in the arrest of Joseph Smith. As *The Globe* reported, "It seems that this turkey, having fears for its immediate future strayed from Smith's place to the farm of Charles Montgomery." Smith apparently made some disparaging remarks about his neighbour, probably accusing him of stealing the bird. When Montgomery caught up with him, angry words were exchanged. A fight ensued, during which Montgomery's ribs were broken. Smith was charged with assault.

Preparing the Christmas bird brought an unexpected bonus to one Ontario woman. It was 1929, and Mrs. J.B. Hammond was dressing the turkey for the family meal. To her surprise, she found a gold nugget in its crop. A local jeweller estimated the nugget to be worth about $2.50 — not a huge amount, but certainly a prize worth having at a time when turkeys sold for around 25 cents a pound. The *Sault Ste. Marie Star* did a bit of investigating and found that the bird was from Manitoba, although no one could pinpoint exactly where in the province it had come from. It had been sold to a wholesale firm in Winnipeg and was then shipped to the Soo.

It wasn't the first turkey to produce a golden nugget. As the newspaper noted, a few years earlier, a turkey owned by George Farmer, who lived just north of the city, "picked up a gold nugget from gravel brought from Root River, and the mineral, as is in this case, was found in the bird's crop."

As far as the turkeys were concerned, both nuggets were simply shiny rocks, just as good for avian digestive processes as any others. Digestion was also on the minds of people who consumed turkeys. Often enough, overindulgence during the holiday season led to upset stomachs. However, there were plenty of remedies available, including a plethora of patent medicines, which were widely advertised in Ontario newspapers and available by mail order or over the counter. In 1863, an advertisement in the *Globe* noted, "Every pleasure has its corresponding sorrow, and Christmas dinners, while so pleasant and palatable, not infrequently produce that very unpleasant sensation known as nightmare, in which the unfortunate dreamer has to combat against legions of turkeys and armies of plum puddings." To alleviate the problem, the ad suggested readers seek out any one of a number of local druggists, who could provide them with a remedy "that will frighten away all the turkeys and plum puddings in Christendom."

Christmas Cheer

Aside from food, an integral part of the holiday is Christmas cheer. Beverages particularly associated with Christmas are mulled wine and mulled cider. Adding sugar and spices to wine and cider then heating them creates warm drinks that are especially welcome in chilly December. Mulled cider is a distant cousin of wassail, from an Anglo-Saxon phrase *waes hael,* which means "be whole" or "hale." In England, it was the custom to raise a toast to apple orchards in the middle of winter in order to ensure a bountiful crop in the coming months. In some areas, a formal procession went from orchard to orchard. In each place, a special tree was selected and some of the drink was sprinkled on its roots while revellers chanted lines commanding the trees to grow.

By the 20th century, wassailing was just a dim and distant memory, probably best known in Christmas carols. Ontarians still had a strong thirst for alcohol at Christmastime, although it was a bit of a trick to satisfy that thirst during the prohibition era. Some turned to non-alcoholic drinks, such as O'Keefe's Dry Ginger Ale, while others found a creative way to stock up on stronger beverages. Because liquor could not be legally sold, except for medicinal purposes, prohibition Christmases usually brought an upsurge in minor ailments. In 1924, the Ontario department of licences estimated that there would be 40,000 more orders placed in the province's dispensaries than there had been in November. Figures from previous years bore out their predictions: in November 1923,

57,715 doctors' prescriptions for liquor had been filled, but in December of the same year, the prescriptions jumped to 87,877. In most cases, each prescription was for a quart of liquor.

"The pressure on the doctors becomes so great about Christmas for prescriptions that they must give in to a certain extent," licence commission spokesman James Hales told a reporter from the *Evening Telegram*. According to a city druggist, the increase had more to do with housewives wanting alcohol for their Christmas plum pudding than drinkers trying to obtain their favourite beverages. But there were plenty who disputed that theory. According to one report, the line-up at a Wellington Street dispensary looked more like the queue in front of the post office. The crowd at the dispensary not only looked pretty healthy, but happy to boot. The reporter who covered the story overheard one businessman explaining he had picked up a cold driving from Hamilton. Apparently his wife had caught the same bug, too.

London also experienced a sudden increase in "sick" people just prior to Christmas; the government dispensary on Talbot Street was doing a booming business! Officials probably knew exactly what was going on, but, as one of them told a *London Free Press* reporter, "It is not up to us to question the sale of liquor made through a bona fide doctor's prescription. Of course, there is a lot of liquor being sold, but as far as we are concerned it is all for medical purposes." Meanwhile, in Windsor, there was a huge upsurge in rum running. From early morning until late at night, trucks and cars brought caseloads of liquor to waiting boats. The boats raced across the river, bringing an estimated extra 40,000 quarts of bootleg booze to thirsty Americans.

Ontarians could also opt for bootleg booze, especially if they did not want to stand in long line-ups at government dispensaries. But there were definite risks. On December 16, a Studebaker owned by a Toronto woman was seized by police. Inside, they found 279 bottles of liquor that were being transported from Montreal. The driver, Joe Simmons, pleaded guilty before a Whitby magistrate on December 23. Convicted, he took three months in jail rather than pay a $600 fine.

Two days after the liquor was confiscated, a reporter for the *Evening Times* conveyed the news of a Toronto magistrate's court with tongue firmly planted in cheek. One of the cases involved John Warden's Royal Edward Hotel on Queen Street West. Beer that exceeded the legal alcohol limits had been found on the premises and Warden was given the choice of a $500 fine or three months in jail. As a result of the sentence, Warden was forced to close the Royal Edward, prompting the Crown Attorney to predict "that all hotels would now become apartment houses." It is doubtful that any of the people present in the courtroom at the time really believed the statement. The writing was already on the wall — prohibition was not working, and, as it turned out, came to an end a short time later. Once again, Ontarians could buy their Christmas cheer with little fuss, although there were still occasional problems.

In 1945, there was a fire in the Lombard Street building in which one of Toronto's liquor stores was located. Apparently caused by an electrical problem, it broke out in a second story business and was quickly stopped after firefighters turned their hoses on it. Meanwhile, business went on as usual in the liquor store. Clerks kept selling and customers kept buying, even though, as one witness reported, water from the fire hoses poured down through the ceiling onto the people in the liquor store. It seems no inconvenience is too great when Ontarians are determined to swallow some seasonal spirit.

Chapter 4
That Jolly Old Elf

A saintly bishop was the inspiration for our modern Santa Claus. St. Nicholas, the story goes, lived in Myra, in southwestern Asia Minor, in the fourth century. A kind-hearted and generous man, he once gave three bags of gold to three noblewomen, providing them with the dowries they needed to marry. A number of miracles were also attributed to him, including one in which he restored three boys to life after an innkeeper had killed them and tried to turn them into bacon. As a result of that miracle, he was made the patron saint of boys and later, of all children.

The name Santa Claus is derived from the Dutch version of his name, Sanct Herr Nicholas, or Sintirklaas. In the early 19th century, he was often portrayed as a tall man in fur-trimmed clothing, usually looking more regal than jolly. Traditionally, he was depicted dressed in red bishop's robes, travelling across the sky as fast as the wind on a white horse. (In some accounts, Sleipnir, the horse, had eight legs and originally belonged to the Germanic god Odin.)

Transplanted to New York State, Dutch traditions became firmly entrenched in North American culture through the work of two writers. One was Washington Irving, who wrote frequently about Santa Claus. The other was Clement Clark Moore, a scholarly man whose poem, *A Visit from Saint Nicholas,* revolutionized the image of Santa. In his poem, most commonly known as *'Twas the Night Before Christmas,* Moore transforms St. Nicholas into a jolly old elf. He becomes smaller and plumper and, instead of travelling by horse, he gets around in a sleigh pulled by eight tiny reindeer — Dasher, Dancer, Prancer, Vixen, Comet, Cupid, Donder, and Blitzen.

Irving and Moore were writing at a time when educational levels were rising, when newspaper readership was growing, and when the newly developed middle-class had more money to spend and more items on which to spend it. All these factors helped entrench the new image of Santa Claus in the public's imagination. Many parents encouraged their children's belief in Santa Claus, partly as a means of extending childhood, but also as a way to maintain discipline in the weeks leading up to Christmas. Meanwhile, there were always a few spoilsports around, including older children who thought it was their duty to tell their younger comrades that Santa was nothing but a pleasant fable.

Virginia O'Hanlon, an eight-year-old American girl, was one of these younger children. In 1897, when she asked her doctor father if there really was a Santa Claus, he suggested that she write to the *New York Sun* for an answer because if she read it in the newspaper, it had to be true. The response she received from editor Francis Pharcellus Church became a classic. "Yes, Virginia, there is a Santa Claus," Church wrote. "He exists as certainly as love and generosity and devotion exist, and you know that they abound and give to your life its highest beauty and joy."

The editorial ran on September 21, 1897, and has probably been carried in dozens of newspapers in Canada and the United States almost every year since. At a later time and place, Virginia's dad might well have recommended a different expert and she might have received a completely different answer. In the 1940s, an Ontario psychiatrist created a furore, not just by denying the existence of Santa Claus, but by insisting that parents were harming their children by encouraging them to believe in him.

George Brock Chisholm (1896–1971) was a doctor and veteran of two world wars. The Oakville native was Canada's federal deputy minister of health when he stirred up the controversy about Santa Claus, stating that, "A child who believes in Santa Claus, who really and literally believes, because his daddy told him so, that Santa comes down all the chimneys in the world on the same night has had his thinking ability permanently impaired if not destroyed."

Canadians were furious at what they saw as an attack on a cherished myth and demanded that Chisholm resign from his cabinet post. Chisholm did not, and the calls for his resignation ended when he was appointed the first director of the World Health Organization (WHO). Far from being a crank, Chisholm was a respected physician who worked on the committee that formed the WHO. At the time, the organization was considered revolutionary because its constitution stressed that health meant more than the absence of disease. It also meant complete physical, mental, and social well-being. Chisholm played such a major role in the establishment of the new organization that he was elected to the position of director by a vote of 46-2.

As a psychiatrist, Chisholm was naturally concerned about mental well-being, including the mental health of children. That mental health, he was convinced, relied partly on children being treated with complete honesty by their parents. Catching their parents in a lie — even a seemingly harmless one about Santa Claus — would, in Chisholm's opinion, be a shattering experience for youngsters. Although some people followed Chisholm's thinking, others were extremely confrontational. In 1954, he described one dinner where another guest attacked him on the topic of Santa Claus. According to Chisholm, the man claimed he had believed in Santa until he was seven and it hadn't done him any harm. Later in the evening, though, he mentioned that he suffered from gastric ulcers and bad nerves. This, as far as the eminent doctor was concerned, simply proved his point. In Chisholm's opinion, children were quite capable of coping with reality. The real harm came when dealing with those who misrepresented reality, thus "crippling their ability to think clearly and honestly."

In spite of Ontarians' growing reliance on child psychology and child-rearing manuals, almost no one was willing to abandon Santa in favour of modern ideas about mental health. Besides, some would argue, at the time Dr. Chisholm was making his recommendations, there was ample proof that children had a solid grasp on reality. In a 1947 article for *Maclean's Magazine*, writer Robert Thomas Allen described a department store Santa at work. Patrick Joseph Murphy had worked for the Robert Simpson Company department store in Toronto since 1931 and, at the time of the interview, had plenty of experience with children and their antics. Although many of them were mesmerized by Murphy's Santa, truly believing he was the genuine article, others weren't so sure. Boys in particular asked all kinds of questions about *other* Santas. Murphy explained that as Santa, he had the power to pop up anywhere he chose at very short notice. However, at least one pair of young skeptics decided to verify that explanation themselves. While one watched, the other ran across the street to Eaton's, then ran back to report that he had seen Santa there. The boy who had been keeping his eye on Murphy then confirmed that the Simpson's Santa had not moved from his seat. When they confronted Murphy, he told them that the other Santa was his brother.

For the most part, the youngsters who stood in line to tell Santa what they wanted for Christmas had no doubts about the credentials of the man in the red velvet suit. Often their mothers helped maintain his persona by quietly slipping notes to Murphy, revealing children's names or other information. Sometimes they enlisted Murphy to help with childish misbehaviour, asking him to suggest to their kids that they stop sucking their thumbs or fighting with siblings.

In full costume, complete with yak-hair wig and beard, Murphy was a convincing Santa Claus — despite a slight Newfoundland accent. Usually he was quick to answer the most pressing questions or could bluff his way out of awkward situations. And, after 16 years as Simpson's Santa — a period that included the Great Depression — he was able to make shrewd assessments about family economics. If youngsters asked him to bring expensive presents, such as electric trains, he would tactfully suggest a less costly alternative.

Here Comes Santa Claus
Patrick Murphy was one of a long line of department store Santa Clauses who dazzled and amused children. In Ontario, the tradition of visiting Santa at a store goes back to the late 1800s. In some cases, he was an invisible presence — one Toronto bookstore billed itself as Santa's depository for gifts. But stores that featured a real live Santa had a definite edge,

especially if his arrival was marked by a special event.

The most special event of all was Eaton's annual Santa Claus parade, which started in 1905. Prior to that time, Santa was enthroned in the Toronto department store's Toyland in the weeks leading up to Christmas, but in the late fall of 1905, a series of Eaton's newspaper advertisements hinted that something extra special was about to happen. Santa was on his way to Toronto from the Far North.

A *Toronto Star* newspaper ad which ran on November 29 announced that Santa's train would arrive at Union Station at 9:59 sharp on Saturday morning. Every child who met St. Nick at the Front Street entrance or greeted him along the route to the store was promised a small memento. Meantime, the ad listed items that youngsters could put on their wish lists — toy pianos, magic lanterns, dolls, wooden horses, and carts, all priced at 25 cents each.

Santa arrived as promised on Saturday, December 2. He was a little later than anticipated, but was still "welcomed royally" by crowds of boys and girls. The float on which he rode was simple — a wagon drawn by a team of horses carrying a red and black checkered packing case that served as Santa's seat. The wagon carried Santa to the store on Yonge Street, where Santa could be visited in Toyland every day from 9 to 10:30 a.m. and from 2:30 to 4 p.m.

Eventually, Eaton's sponsored parades in Montreal, Winnipeg, and Edmonton, but the Toronto event was the first and frequently the most lavish. In the early years, organizers played with Santa's mode of transportation. In 1906, he arrived in a coach drawn by four horses. In 1913, eight live reindeer, brought in from Labrador especially for the occasion, pulled Santa's sled down Yonge Street. Fifteen years later, the parade consisted of eight floats.

By 1955, the year it marked its 50th anniversary, the parade was a mile long, comprised of some 44 floats and 88 nursery rhyme and storybook characters. A full-time staff of carpenters, artists, and paper sculptors were employed year round to plan and implement the event. All kinds of details had to be considered, including municipal regulations. One of the best-loved floats in the Toronto parade at this point featured Mother Goose. However, although the float met Toronto regulations, it was too big to ship by rail to Montreal.

Timing was crucial once the parade got underway. It had to move past any given point within 20 minutes in order to minimize traffic disruptions. Although store employees had once marched in the parade as costumed characters, at this point Toronto high school students were involved. There were also a number of marching bands. By the mid-1950s, walkie-talkies were making it somewhat easier for organizers to communicate, but they still relied on their own eyes and ears to spot any problems. As an additional safety measure, a doctor and nurse, as well as a stand-in, always travelled close to Santa's float.

Starting in 1928, Eaton's employee Jack Brockie headed

Santa Claus in the Eaton's parade, Toronto, Ontario, November 17, 1917.

up the parade arrangements, overseeing all the details that turned the annual event into a cherished Christmas tradition. Brockie had definite ideas about what was appropriate and what was not, leaning heavily towards traditional depictions of holiday themes. Under this management, Santa always arrived in a sleigh pulled by reindeer. New attractions were added only after considerable thought. In the 1950s, one of the most popular was Punkinhead, a tow-headed little bear that had been created by a company copywriter in 1949 to promote a Yuletide giveaway. By the mid-1950s,

Punkinhead was showing up on all kinds of children's merchandise, including T-shirts and mugs.

Preserving a half-century-old tradition in the booming post-war period was a bit of a challenge. As television swept into Ontario homes, there were fears that people would stay in their living rooms rather than risk frigid weather to watch the parade. Some did, although in the early years black-and-white television images were a poor substitute for the vivid colours of the parade. Another concern for parade organizers was the increasing interest in space exploration. In 1955, Jack Brockie told an interviewer, "when space ships and supermen come in, I go out." Four years later, in another article about the parade, Margaret Munnoch stressed that the organizers deliberately steered away from science fiction themes and "have kept rockets, planets, and missiles completely divorced from Santa's Parade." By this time, Sputnik had been launched, and the U.S. was about to become deeply involved in the space race; but to organizers it seemed there was no connection between space and Santa — a Christmas icon from the days before planes, automobiles, and even trains. Yet the integration of holiday tradition and hi-tech travel and communication had already begun.

It started with a typographical error in 1955 when a newspaper in Colorado Springs, Colorado, printed the telephone number of the local Santa Hotline. At least it was supposed to be Santa's number. Instead, callers found themselves connected to the hotline at the Continental

Air Defence Command, the predecessor of NORAD (North American Aerospace Defence Command). When the senior officer on duty took the very first call, he heard a small voice at the other end of the line asking to speak to Santa. Rather than disappoint the owner of the voice, he explained that he was one of Santa's helpers and that he was tracking him on the radar screen as he started his journey from the North Pole. Other calls followed, and the local news media picked up the story. The next year, more children called to find out where Santa Claus was on the radar screen. Caught up in the spirit of the season, military personnel established a tradition of issuing reports on Santa's whereabouts. Eventually, NORAD also established a web site so youngsters could track Santa for themselves.

In 2000, the NORAD site received more than 200 million hits. According to the site, "Santa Cams" located around the world keep an eye on Santa and his reindeer, taking pictures of them as they enter a country and downloading them to a web site so boys and girls can see their progress for themselves. There is also special infrared tracking that can locate Santa and his sleigh by pinpointing the heat from Rudolph's nose.

Along with providing information to anxious children, NORAD's tracking system provides advance information for fighter pilots who form the official escort for Santa and the reindeer. In 2002, those pilots were alerted by the Canadian Air Defence Sector Operations Centre in the underground complex at 22 Wing North Bay, Ontario. Two of the pilots took off from Bagotville, Quebec, to meet Santa as he crossed over Labrador, while a third waited at Cold Lake, Alberta, to escort him out of Canadian airspace. As a courtesy to his escort, Santa always slows down the sleigh so the CF-18 Hornet fighters can keep up with him.

Most of the time, NORAD's Santa watch proceeds without a hitch. But technical problems struck in 2003. A Sudbury boy, eight-year-old Matthew Breczki, was terribly disappointed when, after several attempts, he was unable to track Santa on the web site. His father took action and called NORAD headquarters in Colorado Springs. Major Douglas Martin, deputy director of public affairs, responded by e-mail, saying the technicians were working on it. Apparently three of the Santa Cams were down, but there were hopes that they could be restored to service quickly so that tracking could continue. Eventually, the Santa Cams were back online.

Of course, fighter pilots aren't Santa's only helpers. Generations of children have heard tales of others, including elves who help make toys for good little girls and boys. To assist department store and mall Santas, very large "elves" help out by calming crying children and taking photographs. Then there are those anonymous helpers who function as Santa's secretaries, answering the thousands of letters from hopeful children. Some have regular jobs on the staff of local newspapers. Others are Canada Post employees. Each year, about 13,000 postal elves answer letters addressed to Santa at the North Pole. In 1999, one of the elves apparently was a little late getting into the Christmas spirit. When Jonathon Comeau, a seven-year-old Oshawa boy wrote to Santa asking for a number of presents, he received the standard reply, plus something more. A particularly wicked elf added a postscript to the letter, "You are one greedy little boy." Jonathon and his mother asked for and received an apology from Canada Post. As for the elf, he probably got a lump of coal in his stocking at Christmas.

Chapter 5
Christmas Giving

Giving and receiving gifts has been a significant part of Christmas from time immemorial, inspired by aspects of well-known Christmas stories. The holiday tradition of helping the poor can be traced back to Bethlehem. Joseph was a humble carpenter, not wealthy by any standard, and when he and his pregnant wife, Mary, travelled to the City of David at census time, they were unable to get a room at the inn. As a result, Jesus was born in a stable, and ever since, Christians have made an extra effort to dispense charity in memory of the poor couple and the miraculous child they produced.

In 1860, the St. George Society of Toronto turned a store on King Street into a temporary distribution centre for "Christmas cheer for the poor." Starting at two in the afternoon and continuing until after dark, the English immigrants who belonged to the society gave out 5000 pounds of beef, 10 sheep, 150 bushels of potatoes, 3000 pounds of turnips, 200 cabbages, and 600 loaves of bread, plus vast quantities of flour, tea, coffee and sugar. The *Globe* reported that those who received the donations "belong to all the various nationalities, and the appearance they presented gave striking evidence of the amount of misery which at present prevails in this city."

As immigrants, some of the members of St. George's Society may have known loneliness or want during their first years in Ontario. It seems anyone who has ever experienced a bleak or lonely Christmas, or even imagined one, is willing to help out those in need during the holidays.

One individual who puts charity first at Christmas is Joanne Pettes. She knows firsthand what it is like to do without during the holiday season. In 1993, Joanne and her husband, Bruce, were facing a bleak Christmas. They had been living in Oshawa, but when they heard about a job opportunity for Bruce, they moved with their two young sons to Minden. Then the job fell through. With both of them unemployed, they could barely make ends meet. In desperation, Joanne went to the local food bank. A short while later, the food bank delivered boxes of food, clothing, and toys. Joanne made a promise right then that she would do the same for someone else one day.

Ten years later, back in Oshawa, she tried to keep that

promise. The boys were older, and both she and Bruce were working. Although not wealthy, they were comfortable. So Joanne rounded up a turkey, trimmings, and other items, and set aside some money to buy hats and mitts for needy children. Then she tried to find a suitable family. She started by calling the local newspaper and was told they could not give out names. Instead, they gave her the number of a local charity. For the next several hours, Joanne called one organization after another. In every case, she was told to bring items to the agency office or put them in a drop box. Finally, in frustration, she called the newspaper again.

This time, she was told they could provide the names and contact information for local people in need. The newspaper also sent out a reporter, who wrote about Joanne's experience in Minden and her desire to help someone in Oshawa.

When the article was published, it included Joanne's e-mail address. The result was a flood of requests for assistance — and something extra. A number of people also contacted her to see how they could get involved in making Christmas better for needy families. Joanne passed along the information she had, and several people selected families to help. One man eventually conducted his own toy and clothing drive, providing items to several families.

Choosing just one family to help was difficult, Joanne recalled. She finally settled on a young single mother whose situation had been described by a friend. The woman was attending college, determined to make a better future for herself and her daughter. When she was not studying, she devoted all her time and energy to her child. Joanne, who runs a daycare, told her clients about the young woman and several of them pitched in to help. One donated a bag full of beautiful clothing for the little girl.

The young mother and her daughter were invited to the daycare Christmas party, where Santa gave the little girl a gift. Then Joanne loaded up her car with presents and other goodies and drove them back to their apartment. At a glance, she knew how much they needed a little help at Christmas — the young woman could not even afford to replace lightbulbs in her apartment.

It was, Joanne said, "the most amazing Christmas ever." Along with the other people who helped spread Christmas cheer, she is planning to do it again.

The Kindness of Strangers
Sometimes, strangers provide the best Christmas presents. Shortly before December 25, 2003, a Christmas light ignited the Smith family Christmas tree. As fire swept through the Pembroke area house, the family scrambled to safety. Three-year-old Gerry-Lee Smith watched the flames engulf the home from his parents' car. Despite their best efforts, firefighters from the Tri-Township Fire Department were unable to save the building. The Smiths lost everything, and to young Gerry-Lee, it seemed he might lose Christmas as

well. "How's Santa going to know where to find me?" he asked his parents.

Santa, of course, knows everything, and in this case he had a little help from the fire department. The firefighters fundraising association donated more than $150 for presents for the family. A short time later, Santa appeared at the door of Gerry-Lee's grandmother's house. Although the jolly old elf bore a striking resemblance to fire captain Tim Sutcliffe, Gerry-Lee did not notice. All that mattered was that Santa had found him and had brought gifts as well.

Two years earlier, a Windsor family had a similar experience. On December 15, thieves broke into the home of Trisha Thompson and Frank Simpson, stealing 16 gifts purchased for three-year-old Zackery and four-year-old Mackenzie, as well as food and a television satellite receiver. Payday was several days away and there was no money to buy more gifts. But when the community learned of the family's loss, they made up for the thieves' lack of Christmas spirit. They donated hundreds of dollars, food, and dozens of toys. Overwhelmed by the generosity, the couple replaced the items that had been stolen, then donated the rest, including nine boxes of toys, to other needy families.

For those in need, food and clothing are always much appreciated at Christmastime, but youngsters also need something to play with. A Dryden senior citizen makes sure they get it by spending months restoring toys for Christmas hampers. Gladys Johnson loves dolls and spends most of the year cleaning up old dolls and plush toys. She carefully hand washes the dolls, shampoos their hair, and often makes new clothes for them. The toys come from other people in the community, some of whom have brought garbage bags full of them to her for restoration. Some years, she donates as many as 200 toys to the Christmas Cheer drive.

Many people love to give handmade items at Christmas, but lack the time or skill to make them. Fortunately there are other options, including special craft fairs. Fort Frances has a smaller effort called "Spirit of Christmas" It's a silent auction featuring between 250 and 300 handcrafted items, which typically raises about $15,000 for the local Canadian Cancer Society and the Fort Frances Community Chest.

In the hustle and bustle of preparing for December 25, generosity may be temporarily forgotten, but it usually takes just a little nudge to remind people of those less fortunate. A week before Christmas 2001, the Salvation Army in Wallaceburg had only 80 toys to distribute to needy children. But there were 300 children on the list. Many people were facing a difficult Christmas because of layoffs at area companies. Still, it took just one request and the organization had more than enough toys to fill their Christmas hampers.

Organized charities are not the only ones that help the needy at Christmas. In Sarnia, an activist group called Grinch Enterprises kidnapped Santa in 1999 — not the real Santa, but a plywood image that stood in the front yard of Evelyn Hussey. In its place, they left a large note asking for canned food. To prove Santa was still safe, they sent a photograph of him standing on a beach with palm trees in the background.

As a result of the kidnappers' demand, 700 cans of food were donated to a local food bank. Santa was returned unharmed. But a few years later, Grinch Enterprises struck again, and once more the kidnappers demanded food donations.

Christmas Treasures

Part of the tradition of Christmas is the story of the Magi, the three wise kings who followed the Star of Bethlehem to the stable and found the Christ Child. According to tradition, they presented him with costly gifts of gold, frankincense, and myrrh. The Christmas custom of giving gifts evolved in imitation of the wise men's gifts. Practised in the Old World for centuries, it transplanted easily to Ontario.

In 1841, Harriet Jukes spent her first Christmas in Canada near Port Maitland, at the mouth of the Grand River. Harriet, daughter of a captain in the Royal Navy, had recently married Mark Jukes, whose mother, Georgina, and stepfather, Frederick Hyde, had built their Canadian home, Glasserton, a few years earlier. After the 1837 rebellion, they moved back to England temporarily, then returned to Canada in 1841.

Christmas was a beautiful winter day, cold and clear, with a pristine blanket of snow covering the landscape. Harriet, Mark, and the family went off to morning services at Christ's Church, then returned to Glasserton to open presents. They had deliberately put off opening a wooden box shipped from Harriet's family in England until Christmas. Mark pried the box open with a hammer and chisel and the couple carefully unpacked the presents. Harriet began to cry as she opened the items that had been lovingly wrapped by her family in England. There was a muffler for Mark, hand-made clothes for the baby Harriet was expecting, plus hand-knitted socks and various other items, including some flower seeds for spring planting.

The idea of presents is common to most cultures. J.E. Parsons, who taught English to new Canadians in 1960, wrote about his experiences in *Saturday Night* magazine. In his opinion, Christmas was one time of year when national differences were easily transcended. No matter where they came from, most of the Europeans he taught had a good grasp of the idea of Christmas gifts and cards. But, given cultural and language differences, there were some accidentally hilarious moments, including the year his class presented him with a gift and a card which read "Shower Gift for the Bride." On another occasion, the card listed everyone who had given money towards Parsons' Christmas gift — including the amount of each donation!

That Perfect Gift
Finding the right gift can sometimes be difficult, but advertisers are usually more than willing to help. Although we tend to think of the commercialization of Christmas as a modern

phenomenon, it goes back to at least the mid-1800s and the increased availability of newspapers. In 1863, advertisements in Toronto's *Globe* recommended clothing, millinery, cutlery, and books, but noted, "Jewellery, toys and fancy goods are what the public most enquire about on such occasions as this."

By 1904, some of the gifts advertisers suggested included books and carpet sweepers, housecoats, handkerchiefs, and shirts. Good toys for boys included skates, hockey sticks, air guns, and pocketknives. For those with a little more money to spend, there was always the option of Edison phonographs. And for loved ones with a sweet tooth, candy was always a welcome present.

Twenty years later, gifts advertised in Toronto newspapers included linen place mats, silk and kid gloves for women, as well as mirrors, fountain pens, and curling irons. For children, there were all kinds of toys, including teddy bears selling at 98 cents, baby sleighs for $2.65, and Meccano sets at various prices. For those who wanted to buy more lavish gifts, $14.75 could purchase an "English pendant barometer." Slightly more expensive was a 97-piece white and gold dinner set for $16.95. For something really extravagant, there was always the option of a nine-piece walnut dining suite — six chairs, a buffet, a china cabinet, and a table cost just $141.95. Or what about a new car? "Exceed Their Expectations," a large 1924 read. "The gift of a Ford car is the surest way to arouse that Christmas ecstasy."

Ulterior Motives

Arousing that Christmas ecstasy may mean different things to different people. In some cases, gifts are given not simply as a token of affection, but are chosen to provoke a specific reaction from the recipient. In Victorian times, women often embroidered slipper tops or worked them in needlepoint, then had a local shoemaker finish them off as gifts for special friends or relatives. Just before Christmas 1884, a shoemaker in Kingston had a lovely array of homemade slippers on display. Commenting on this, the *British Whig* observed, "When a pretty girl unfolds some of her needle work, and, slyly looking around to see that nobody is within hearing says, 'Make these up on a No. 7 last,' you can just bet that she is anxious to have some young man settle his courting about Christmas." After the shoemaker shaped the size seven slipper on his last and attached the embroidered top, the girl would present the slippers to her beau at Christmas. Because Victorians considered gifts of clothing very personal, the slippers sent a clear message to the young man that he should propose — and soon!

Courting of another kind may have been the motivation for some shoppers discussed by young Toronto saleswomen in 1935. According to a *Daily Mail and Empire* article, the favourite customers of the city's shop girls were "middle-aged fat men" who were well-dressed and carried a walking cane. When these men appeared in stores, the salesgirls flocked around because they were usually big spenders. Younger men would spend just $10 on gifts, and women often spent considerably less, but the middle-aged male shoppers had plenty of money to burn. And they were usually open to the sales clerks' suggestions.

"What do they buy?" repeated one "slim young thing" in response to a reporter's question. "Why, everything we tell them to."

A day earlier, the shop girl had sold a $10 bracelet to a middle-aged man, then suggested a necklace to go with it. He agreed, purchased one for $18, then, after another suggestion or two, bought more jewellery, spending a total of more than $50. With many Ontarians earning less than $500 per year, that was a tremendous amount to spend on gifts.

Possibly this was the reason that middle-aged women, who presumably were more familiar with household budgets, might spend an hour mulling over the purchase of a 50 cent pin, only to return it the next day. The middle-aged men never exchanged items, and their free-spending habits made them extremely popular with salesclerks working on commission. Even when they purchased toys for their grandchildren or nieces and nephews, they were more extravagant than other shoppers. But, the girls noted, their tastes were quite different from those of grandmothers, who wanted the more modern looking dolls, including Shirley Temple dolls, which were extremely popular that year. Grandfathers, on the other hand, were suckers for fancy, overdressed dolls. "The middle-aged men want the doll with the most ribbons and lace on it, and they'll buy the most expensive we have."

Sometimes grandparents were far from practical. In an age before synthetic fabrics, most winter clothing was made of silk or wool. Grandparents invariably picked out the silk items first, although most sales girls conscientiously tried to persuade them that woollen items would be far more appropriate for young children. In contrast, it was children's aunts who seemed to be most in tune with what was appropriate and what would truly delight their nieces and nephews. One salesclerk reported that aunts would buy machine guns for their nephews, even though Auntie might really like toy dogs better. They also knew, that Christmas of 1935, that Buck Rogers and G-men toys were guaranteed to please the little fellows in the family. Those aunts had mastered one of the main techniques of Christmas giving: put yourself in the shoes of the recipient.

That Christmas Rush

Christmas shopping can be a frustrating experience, especially when the perfect gift is in short supply. One example of this was the Cabbage Patch Dolls that were popular in the early 1980s. The 41-centimetre stuffed dolls were actually soft sculptures, each of them unique. It seemed every young girl just had to have one, and parents stood in line for hours at stores or paid exorbitant prices to private individuals in order to get the dolls. Sometimes, shoppers' Christmas spirit completely disappeared in their anxiety to acquire the dolls.

Christmas Giving

In Windsor, more than 1000 people rushed into one store when a supply of the dolls arrived. Several swore at one shopper who cut into a line-up, and one man threatened to throw an annoying child through a shop window. In Cambridge, when 500 people showed up at a store that had advertised 48 Cabbage Patch dolls for sale, police had to be called in to keep order. Similar scenes were repeated all across Ontario. The frenzy had a lot more to do with status than with the spirit of Christmas — and may also have involved a little bit of greed. Humans are acquisitive by nature and sometimes carry their desire to obtain items to ridiculous lengths. Modern experts may rant about materialism at Christmas, but it is really nothing new, and, besides, it can provide a little bit of humour during the holidays.

Take, for instance, an item which appeared in Kingston's *British Whig Standard* on Christmas Eve 1884. Although it reads like a poem, it was not set out line by line, like typical poetry. Instead, a typesetter printed the lines so they would form the shape of a stocking and placed it on the front page of the paper so it would immediately attract the readers' attention. It began:

"Dear Santa Claus," wrote little Will in letters truly shocking. "I've been a good boy, so please fill a heapen in my stocking. I want a drum to make pa sick and drive my mamma crazy. I want a doggy I can kick so he will not get lazy. I want a powder gun to shoot right at my sister Annie, and a big trumpet I can toot just awful loud at granny.

The fictional Will also wanted a mask to scare the baby, a pony to race around the parlour, and a hatchet to chop up the grand piano. Whoever composed the piece was probably all too familiar with high-spirited little boys, or perhaps had seen his sons get one inappropriate present too many from other adults.

The Mind of a Child

Sometimes adults are very well meaning but simply cannot fathom the mind of a child. One Christmas present that did not work out quite the way it was planned was a hamster purchased by a Dryden newspaper editor. Typically, fathers play Santa to their kids on Christmas Eve, drinking the milk and cookies left out for them and perhaps leaving large footprints in strategic locations. As a single mother, Laurie Papineau had to take on this role herself. One Christmas, she didn't get around to that pleasant duty until 2 a.m. Christmas morning. That's when she discovered that Delaney, her seven-year-old daughter, had left a note for Santa. Since her pet hamster had died just two days earlier, Laurie expected Delaney to ask for a replacement and had secretly purchased a new one. But the request specifically asked Santa *not* to bring a hamster, out of respect for the dear departed rodent. Instead, could Santa put a candy cane on the dead hamster's grave?

Laurie hesitated. The hamster was buried in a clearing in the woods three-quarters of a kilometre away. The spot was selected because it was the only piece of ground that wasn't frozen. The family had located a small burrow, put in the hamster, and topped it up with four bags of cat litter.

It was dark and cold outside. Laurie hesitated, but her older children, then in their late teens, reminded her she would have gone outside for them when they were Delaney's age. Laurie gritted her teeth, grabbed a flashlight and candy cane, and headed into the darkness. It was freezing cold. Trees and bushes blocked the way, scratching Laurie as she pushed on. Then the flashlight went out. But she still managed to find her way to the tiny grave, deposit the candy cane, and stumble back through the bush before collapsing into bed in the wee small hours of the morning.

The next morning, the first thing Delaney did after getting up was put on her jacket and run out to check the hamster's grave. There was the candy cane, along with an unexpected addition. Santa had left a note, thanking Delaney for giving her departed hamster such a loving home and asking her to adopt a new one. The replacement hamster was accepted happily, and Delaney's faith in Santa remained unshaken.

Chapter 6
Holiday Hazards

I n 1855, the editor of Brantford's *Expositor, Railway Advocate and General Advertiser* wrote, "Christmas is a season of festivity and happiness. Many congregate together to spend the day in the most hilarious manner, each striving to make the other happy, and all contributing to throw such a fascinating spell around the scene as makes it highly congenial to human nature."

Christmas is supposed to be a time for luxury and a little indulgence. But not all Christmases can be described as congenial, or even comfortable. When things don't turn out the way they are supposed to, the only thing to do is make the best out of a rather difficult situation, especially if circumstances are beyond one's control.

Holiday Hazards

On December 24, 1986, the Ottawa Valley, parts of eastern Ontario, and southwestern Quebec were hit with a severe ice storm. Freezing rain fell for nearly 14 hours, creating heavy accumulations that resulted in power outages. By Christmas Day, something like one in four residents of the area was without electricity. Determined to celebrate regardless of the power problems, many households cooked their holiday turkeys on the barbecue.

That was a minor inconvenience compared to those suffered by early Ontario residents. For some pioneers, Christmas 1837 was a difficult one. The holiday fell shortly after William Lyon Mackenzie led the rebellion in Upper Canada. Although government troops had quickly suppressed the uprising, rumours were still flying about the province in late December. The result in some communities, including Ancaster, west of Hamilton, was that people stayed away from services at the Anglican Church. According to Reverend John Miller, there were "only about 50 persons present at church" on Christmas Day 1837.

A few years later, Nathaniel Parker Willis (1806–1867) wrote about a particularly rough time experienced by two men shortly before Christmas. Willis, one of a myriad of writers who described the exotic wilderness of Canada in the 1800s, was in the Talbot settlement, near London and Nissouri Townships around 1840. Two weeks before Christmas, two hunters, Howay and Nowlan, went off in search of a bear. They stalked the beast for some 32 kilometres, but had not caught up to him as night fell. So they camped for the night, along with their dog. The next morning, they breakfasted on the crumbs left over from the meal they had brought with them, sharing part of it with their dog, then set off after the bear again.

By the end of the day, they realized they were lost and decided to head back towards the settlement. But they had become completely confused. Over the next several days, their situation went from bad to worse. Although they walked almost constantly all day long, they seemed to get no closer to any kind of settlement. They were out of food, frequently thirsty, usually cold, and one night, Nowlan's feet froze. Although they managed to shoot one partridge, it was hardly enough to satisfy them.

On the seventh day, their dog collapsed. The men were so hungry that they thought they were capable of eating any-thing, but they were reluctant to make a meal out of the dog that had stayed by them during their ordeal. Instead, they abandoned the animal and continued on their trek, con-vinced they could find their way out by following a stream. But poor visibility and a swampy area set them off course again. Soon they realized they were walking in circles.

Meanwhile, a search party had been organized; some of the "best dogs in the country" were rounded up, and several men of the Talbot District set off with compasses and trum-pets, calling for the missing hunters as they scoured "thou-sands of acres of interminable forests and desolate swamps."

A light snow, which might have provided some help in tracking the missing pair, melted during a sudden thaw, making the search even more difficult. Finally, after two days, the search party gave up and returned to their homes, convinced the missing men were dead. The only consolation they had, Willis wrote, was that they were "men without families — they were strangers in America" and no one except some "unconnected neighbours" would be left to mourn them.

As far as Howay and Nowlan were concerned, they might as well have been dead. Panicked, starving, and completely despondent, the men were ready to give up all hope. But they headed once more for a river, and this time they heard what sounded like a cowbell. They followed it, discovered a log cabin, which, to their great surprise, turned out to be inhabited. They were 80 kilometres from home at this point, half-starved, and suffering from exposure, but a little food and some nursing put them in good enough condition to make the journey home. To the surprise of everyone in the settlement, including Nathaniel Willis, they returned on Christmas Day.

No Food for the Feast

The harrowing experience of the two hunters was not too far removed from that of many early Ontario pioneers. Although wild berries and game were plentiful in the Ontario backwoods, knowing which ones to gather or how to hunt successfully was a skill that many early settlers lacked. In addition, some of them, especially the more genteel settlers, preferred to eat familiar foods, even if they paid a high price for them. Writing anonymously around 1871, an "emigrant lady" described how her son provided a chicken and some mutton on Christmas Day. Although he paid a good price for it, the chicken was so thin that its bones were sticking out of its skin, and the women of the household were convinced that if it had not been butchered it would have soon died of consumption. In spite of the meagre size of the chicken, the emigrant lady added butter, onions, and spices, and "concocted a savoury stew which was much applauded." The woman also managed to produce a pudding, which was long on flour, short on currants and grease, and completely devoid of plums, sugar, spice, eggs, citron and brandy. The lady remarked, "the less said about that pudding the better."

Food was not the only difficulty. The emigrant lady, the widow of a British officer, had spent 15 years in Calais, France, until forced to leave in the aftermath of the Franco-German War. Although she was happy to be with the family in the Muskoka cabin, her thoughts naturally wandered back to happier, more prosperous times. She worried that all their efforts in the new land might never pay off, but, for the sake of the rest of the group, "I tried to simulate a cheerfulness I was far from feeling, and so we got over the evening. We had a good deal of general conversation, and some of our favourite songs were sung by the gentlemen."

Despite the brave face she put on things, the family's

situation in Canada did not improve. Christmas 1874 rolled around anyway. Very early that morning, the lady heard a cheerful shout and looked out to see her son Charles coming towards the cabin. With him he brought two very small salt herring and a large vegetable marrow. This was all he could contribute to the family's fourth Christmas dinner in Canada. Food shortages or not, the group prepared to celebrate. Charles was sent to retrieve his wife and two children, while someone else borrowed some butter from a neighbour, who was also invited for dinner. The feast that evening was mashed vegetable marrow, mashed potatoes, "well buttered, peppered, salted and baked in the oven," two herring, and plenty of tea. For dessert there were dampers — hot flour biscuits. And everyone dressed in their best for Christmas: "Cinderella transformations were not more complete. My daughter became the elegant young woman she has always been considered; my sons, in once more getting into their gentlemanly clothes, threw off the careworn look of working-day fatigue, and became once more distinguished and good-looking young men; and as to my pretty daughter-in-law, I have left her till the last to have the pleasure of saying that I never saw her look more lovely. She wore a very elegant silk dress, had delicate lace and bright ribbons floating about her, a gold locket and chain and sundry pretty ornaments, relics of her girlish days, and to crown all her beautiful hair flowing over her shoulders."

But even with the brave attempt, no one tried to sing

that Christmas Day, not even the favourite hymns that had sustained the family in the past. The year had been far too difficult. The family had little food and less money. The wheat crop, which they hoped would partially alleviate their problems, was damaged by harsh weather. Although she had enjoyed some previous success, the emigrant lady's attempts to earn money through her writing met with rejection after rejection. Worried about the health of her eldest son, who seemed to be growing thinner each month, she made up her mind to find a way to return to England. Her first attempt failed because of lack of money. Hiding her disappointment as best she could, she settled in for another miserable winter in the bush. Fortunately, a glimmer of hope came with the New Year, when a kindly neighbour provided the family with a wild turkey. The situation continued to improve — friends in Britain loaned the family enough money to enable them to leave Muskoka. On March 2, 1875, with absolutely no regrets, the emigrant lady and her family left behind their wilderness home forever.

Runaway Deer
A minor holiday crisis occurred in Toronto in December 1924. As two street cleaners were travelling up Church Street one morning they spotted a deer dodging a streetcar. Concerned about the animal, they shooed it into a small lane then cornered it in a backyard. Although their first thought was probably that it was a wild deer that had somehow

wandered into the city, the two cleaners soon discovered that the animal was quite tame. Within no time at all it was taking bread from their hands.

Meanwhile, the owner of the yard called the humane society. An inspector paid a visit and tried to take the four-year-old buck into custody. The deer refused to co-operate, butting the inspector in the head and hands and cutting him up quite badly. Finally the inspector, who seems to have had a bit of cowboy blood in him, threw the deer down and roped its legs together.

Further investigation revealed that the deer belonged to one T.B. Tough of Jarvis Street, who had bought it in Niagara Falls when it was still a fawn. Normally it was kept in the yard of a local hotel, close to Tough's residence, but apparently it had decided to do a bit of wandering all on its own. The newspaper report provides no information on the ultimate fate of the deer, or whether the humane society inspector spent his Christmas telling how his job description included wrangling reindeer.

Wartime Christmas

For many Ontarians, the most difficult Christmases have been during wartime, especially during the First and Second World Wars. In both instances, food was rationed, making it difficult to obtain the sugar, butter, and other items essential to holiday goodies. More importantly, loved ones were often far away, so instead of joy and togetherness, Christmas was filled with longing and fear. Even after the soldiers came home there were difficulties, including housing shortages and problems adjusting to family members who were virtual strangers after years of separation.

All the same, just about everyone was smiling in 1945 as many soldiers returned from the war. Fairly typical was the arrival of the Queen's Own Rifles, who reached Toronto on December 17, 1945. Lieutenant-Colonel Stephen Lett, the commanding officer, was greeted by his English bride, who had already been in Canada for five months. Other soldiers were met by parents, siblings, wives, and children. For one soldier, the homecoming was extra special. Prior to the war, the parents of Regimental Sergeant Major Ted Hartnell had been living in western Canada and he had not seen them for nine years prior to joining up. After four years of wartime service that took him to the beaches of Normandy and made him a Member of the Order of the British Empire, Ted came home to find his parents had moved to Toronto. When his regiment was dismissed, he hurried to their Belgravia Avenue home, where he found his parents, his wife, and the young son he had never met. "Who says there's no Santa Claus?" he asked.

Yet amid the smiles and warm welcomes, there were problems. The same newspaper that carried the story of Ted Hartnell's return also reported that Torontonians should prepare for a temporary shortage of coal. At the time, most of the coal consumed in the city was shipped by rail from Buffalo, but a series of storms had delayed deliveries. They were also told to expect turkey shortages. With so many military personnel returning from overseas, the demand had increased to a point where suppliers were unable to keep up. Some measures were being taken to stretch the supply, however. Under regulations that stipulated prisoners of war could not receive goods that were being rationed for civilians, government authorities declared that Japanese and German prisoners of war still interned in Canada would not receive turkeys for their Christmas dinner. Meanwhile, authorities were also making arrangements for Canadian servicemen who were still stationed overseas to get turkey and all the trimmings for their holiday meals.

At least one returned serviceman had already feasted on turkey and was planning to do it again. In fact, he was determined to absolutely stuff himself over the holidays. William Kinmond, a reporter for the *Toronto Star*, had spent four years as a prisoner of war in Germany. Now safely back in Canada, he described Christmas meals that could hardly be thought of as festive. One year, the prison-camp cooks tried to make the usual fare of turnips look better by adding a broth made from bones and water. It still looked like bones and water, but a few of the bones had some marrow left in them. The lucky prisoners who found some of those bones in their bowls took them back to their bunks to suck on them as long as they could.

Christmas 1944 at the camp was better than most.

Kinmond and his fellow prisoners were wakened by a newly arrived American captive who presented them each with a cigarette and a cup of ersatz coffee. Meanwhile, the cook had scrounged what supplies he could, and the meals served that day were better than the usual menu. Lunch was a soup made of peas and potatoes, although it was so thin that Kinmond commented, "without the peas we would have had three potatoes and a cup of hot water." Dinner was a stew made of some mysterious meat. There was even some dessert, thanks to the ingenuity of the men who hoarded supplies, including Red Cross rations of raisins, prunes, sugar, and biscuits. By combining these with water and whatever butter or milk they could find and cooking them in a powdered milk tin, the men were able to produce little cakes. Most were pitifully small, just a bite or two at best, but the more talented chefs made their cakes look very nice. Some even coloured the milk-powder icing with beet juice and used it to write Christmas messages across the top of their cakes.

By 1945, although he was still terribly thin, William Kinmond had put those lean days behind him and was looking forward to Christmas dinner. Lots of Christmas dinner. "There'll be no ersatz coffee or pea soup or mystery stew on the Christmas that is to come," he vowed. "The ghost of Christmas past can only spur me on to greater efforts and a stomach ache will only be an indication of successful eating."

Holiday Hazards

Number, Please

Sitting down to Christmas dinner with family and friends is one of the main pleasures of Christmas Day. But every year there are a number of people who cannot do this, or who have to cut their celebrations short because of work obligations. In 1935, Toronto telephone operators were among those who spent Christmas at work.

Kevin W. MacTaggart, a reporter for the Toronto *Mail and Empire*, visited the main telephone exchange on Adelaide Street on Christmas night. The long room, located on the 10th floor of a building, was filled with female operators, all ready to handle the calls that started to flood in when lower long distance rates went into effect at 7 p.m. They and other telephone employees had been preparing for more than a month for the busiest telephone time of the year. In a single hour that night, 14,300 calls came in and another 1000 went out.

As MacTaggart explained, everyone wanted to call family and friends on Christmas, and when they did they wanted to talk. It was the telephone operators' responsibility to connect them to the right party and to make sure they knew when their calls went over the initial three minutes.

In the days before automated phone systems, it took a lot of highly trained people to accomplish this. Those people had to have considerable stamina, because the calls came in steadily for five hours. Seconds after 7 p.m., the switchboard lit up and it stayed that way until midnight.

Back in 1935, there were no pre-recorded messages, no computers to assist operators. Callers asked all kinds of questions — what time it was, what the weather was like, how much it would cost them to call a tiny town halfway across the continent. Operators were not only expected to provide the information, but to do so quickly and pleasantly. As MacTaggart discovered, they did this with the help of a lot of support staff, including the "rating" and "routing" girls who provided essential information to the operators. If a caller wanted to speak to someone in a tiny British Columbia town, for instance, a Toronto operator might not be sure how to connect the call. So she wrote out a ticket, put it on the back of her chair, and one of several runners working the room picked it up. The ticket was taken to a routing girl, who provided the information, then the runner got it back to the operator and the customer was connected. Similarly, if a caller wanted to know how much it would cost to talk to a family friend in a tiny village in the Maritimes, the operator would fill out a ticket and one of the rating girls would quickly come up with the answer.

It was a high-pressure job, made more difficult on Christmas night because of the volume and because some of the callers had been celebrating all day. But MacTaggart came away impressed by the quiet efficiency of the operators whose well manicured hands moved deftly, constantly connecting lines in the huge switchboard so that

Holiday Hazards

Torontonians could share their Christmas with family and friends far away.

Chapter 7
Spirit of the Season

Christmas brings out the best in people. For at least one day of the year, almost everyone makes the effort to get along. The idea of peace on earth and good will towards all prevails, and it can make a huge difference in how individuals treat one another.

Sometimes, the spirit of Christmas goes far beyond a little generosity. In 2001, 17-year-old Ian Duffey woke early Christmas morning to find a fire raging through his grandmother's townhouse in Scarborough. Waking his 18-year-old sister, he told her to climb through the window and get help. Then he ran to his grandmother's bedroom and helped her out of the second-storey window.

Ian's 14-year-old sister was still in the house, and

despite dense, choking smoke, he struggled to her bedroom in an attempt to rescue her. Tragically, he was overcome by smoke and both he and his sister died in the fire. His courage won him a posthumous Medal of Bravery.

Heroism comes in many forms. Canadian actor and musician Tom Jackson knows about hunger and homelessness at Christmas. After leaving home at 15, he spent several years on the streets of Winnipeg. After launching a successful career, the *North of 60* star made up his mind to reach out to the less fortunate. In 1987, he held the first Huron Carole benefit concert in Toronto. The following year he established the Christmas and Winter Relief Association, a non-profit association whose mandate is to raise money for organizations that deal directly with homeless Canadians. The main fundraiser for the association has been the Huron Carole concert, which, by the year 2000, was making 15 stops across Canada, including performances in Ottawa and Hamilton. Top Canadian artists, such as Susan Aglukark, Dan Hill, Prairie Oyster, Moxy Fruvous, and the Rankin Sisters, are among those who have performed over the years. Supported by free print and media advertising, the Huron Carole benefit has helped raised millions of dollars for food banks.

Christmas Reunion

Reaching out to others is an integral part of Christmas. Sometimes it is simply a matter of gathering together to celebrate or share memories. Sometimes, reaching out takes the form of patching up old quarrels and starting afresh. And sometimes it means finding family members after long years of separation.

That is precisely what happened to one English family. After their mother died in 1927, Fred Paul and his siblings were separated. Fred's stepfather, Albert Clark, could not care for his three stepsons, Alfred (14), Fred (13), and Ernie (11), along with his own young children, Bert and Ethel. So the older boys were sent to Dr. Barnardo's Home in London, England. Barnardo's charity specialized in sending British "home children" to Canada, where, it was thought, the fresh air and wide-open spaces would improve their health and offer more opportunities for them to escape the grinding poverty experienced by many working-class families. However, the system was flawed, and like many home children, the Paul boys were badly treated by their Canadian foster families. Alfred eventually settled in Toronto, and Fred lived in Muskoka and Millgrove, near Hamilton. Ernie became a policeman in Sudbury, but was shot and killed in 1955. Meanwhile, Bert and Ethel Clark, the boys' half-brother and sister, were also separated and lost track of each other for 30 years. They finally reconnected in 1982.

Through all these years, the siblings kept looking for one another, consulting missing persons bureaus and police stations, running newspaper advertisements, and asking for help from anyone who might be able to give it. In 1984, a friend of the Pauls spotted an advertisement in a Sudbury newspaper, placed by someone seeking information about the family. When this friend told Ernie's widow about the ad, she passed the information along to Fred, who made a call to England. After nearly 60 years, the siblings had found each other.

Ironically, Bert and Fred had actually crossed paths during the Second World War. At the time, Fred was serving with the Hastings and Prince Edward Regiment. When they disembarked in Scotland, Bert was there to pipe the troops ashore, but the half-brothers did not recognize each other.

As a result of the newspaper ad and phone call, Bert and Ethel boarded a plane for the first time in their lives and flew to Canada for an extended Christmas vacation with their brothers. To make sure Fred would recognize them at the Toronto airport, they each wore a red rose.

There were tears of joy when the siblings met again after nearly seven decades apart. There was sorrow, too, when Ethel and Bert learned of Ernie's death. But for the four remaining siblings, nothing could really overshadow the happiness of the reunion. As Ethel told a Hamilton *Spectator* reporter, "It shows you can never have enough hope or faith."

Christmas Miracles

When a child is sick, hope and faith is often all parents have to rely on. When a child dies, it is a tragedy, especially if the death occurs close to Christmas. But sometimes miracles of hope and faith bring a measure of peace.

Christmas in Ontario

Shortly before Christmas 1984, three-year-old Gordie Lock of Hamilton was riding in his father's cab. When the taxi turned a corner, the door suddenly flew open. Gordie flew out, fell to the curb, and was struck by another car. He was rushed to McMaster University Medical Centre, where doctors told Paul and Dianne Lock that their son was brain dead. Struggling through their grief, the couple decided to donate Gordie's organs.

Meanwhile, in Louisville, Kentucky, five-year-old Amie Garrison was slowly dying of liver disease. Biliary atresia, a birth defect, prevented her liver from functioning properly, and her body was slowly shutting down. Her parents had been trying for years to find a liver for her and, to increase the chances of locating one, had publicized her plight. Just a week before Gordie's accident, Amie had been invited to the White House to place a star atop a Christmas tree, an event that was televised nationally.

The donation of Gordie's organs made Amie's survival possible. In a lengthy operation, the Ontario boy's liver was transplanted into the body of the American girl. Amie responded well to the surgery. Two days later, the families were in touch. Although donors are usually anonymous, as soon as they made the decision to donate their son's organs, Paul and Dianne Lock contacted the media. They wanted to focus attention on the need for transplant organs. The ensuing publicity made it easy for Teresa Garrison, Amie's mother, to reach the Hamilton couple after the girl's operation. The long distance chats resulted in a meeting a few weeks later and a friendship developed between the families of the two children.

Knowing that part of their son survived in Amie helped the Locks come to terms with Gordie's death. For Amie and her family, the new organ was the best Christmas gift of all. As a result of the operation, Amie grew into adulthood and eventually had a little boy of her own.

Peaceful Wishes in Wartime

For A.F. Kemble of Toronto, evidence of the spirit of Christmas was clearly demonstrated in a German prisoner of war camp during the First World War. In 1917, the Toronto man's third Christmas in prison was approaching. The first two holidays had been no different from any other days in the camp. But the third was special because of the efforts of one man, a German officer.

Shortly before Christmas, the prisoners received an invitation to a Christmas party. At the time they were skeptical — after three years surrounded by barbed war and bayonets, they had little reason to trust their captors. But, more from curiosity than anything else, they accepted the invitation.

When they awoke on Christmas morning, two surprises greeted them. First, all the guards were unarmed. And secondly, right in front of the guardhouse was a huge Christmas tree, dripping with tinsel and dozens of presents. The prisoners were asked to gather round the tree. Then the camp commandant spoke, telling the men how much he regretted that the war had taken them so far from home and family at Christmas, and how he hoped that the gulf between the two warring nations would eventually disappear after peace. He also asked that the men say nothing about the Christmas party in their letters home as he was acting without the permission of his superior officers.

For the rest of the day, he told the men, discipline would be relaxed. He trusted they would not attempt to escape. He also informed them that they could buy as much wine from the canteen as they wanted. As he finished his speech, a small gramophone started to play "Silent Night" and the commandant began to remove small presents from the tree, passing them out to each man.

The prisoners responded with three cheers and a rousing rendition of "For he's a jolly good fellow." Then, taking their gifts with them, they went back to their barracks. Most were convinced the commandant's conciliatory gesture meant the war must be winding down.

As it was, the war dragged on for another 10 months, until November 1918. And, just a month after the Christmas party, the camp commandant was suddenly replaced by "a hard-boiled scoundrel." But, 20 years later, Kemble vividly remembered the other commandant and the Christmas of 1917: "I for one will always have a kindly feeling for this German officer who was not afraid to step from behind the great false face of hate that nation presents to nation in time of war and show his true features to us in recognition of the all-embracing kinship of Christmas Day."

How can you celebrate when loved ones are so far from home and in grave danger? How do you deal with Christmas carols and cards wishing "peace on earth" when war is raging? In December 1939, shortly after the start of the Second World War, the wife of Canada's governor-general addressed those questions. In an article for *Saturday Night,* Lady Tweedsmuir urged Canadian parents to celebrate Christmas in as normal a fashion as possible for the sake of their children. Speaking of the "awful feeling of insecurity" that war created, she pointed out that despite their parents' best efforts, children would hear about the horrors of war and worry about it. "They feel that nothing is safe, everything is rocking round them. At any moment their father, brother or schoolmaster may be taken by this monster whose fiery breath fans their cheek," she wrote. But Christmas, she continued, provided the security of familiar and cherished traditions, "a festival of the church, spiritual and joyous, something warm and human and generous, a light which nothing can put out!"

As for "peace on earth, goodwill to men," Lady Tweedsmuir suggested the historic lines be taken as a challenge, an impetus for parents to spend the rest of their lives fighting the causes of war, poverty, and racism. The present might have seemed gloomy and threatening, but she maintained it could also encourage people to "put our hopes for the future into our singing, and pray fervently that our children may live in an age in which peace and goodwill reign on earth."

Operation Santa Claus

In effect, Lady Tweedsmuir was trying to persuade Canadians to carry the Christmas spirit through the rest of the year. That's a difficult undertaking for many, but there are some people who make the attempt. One of the most celebrated is Jimmy Lomax of Hamilton.

As a young child, Jimmy developed a serious lung disease and spent many months in hospital. Doctors predicted the ailment would kill him before he was out of his teens. But they were wrong. An encounter with Santa Claus changed his life.

When Jimmy realized that Santa was just an ordinary man dressed up in costume, he was amazed. He vowed that if he lived he would put on a Santa costume himself and do whatever he could to make sick children happy at Christmastime.

To the surprise of medical experts, Jimmy recovered. And he kept his promise. At 15, he persuaded a gas station owner to give him five dollars to buy candy for sick and needy kids at Christmas. To stretch the money, he bought leftover Halloween goodies. Then he put on a Santa Claus suit made by a local schoolteacher and went door to door, giving candy to children who were facing the prospect of a less than wonderful Christmas.

That was in 1958. Jimmy grew up and went to work at Stelco, the steel mill that is one of Hamilton's major employers. The money was good, but the job was not particularly prestigious — at one time Jimmy described himself as a "flunky from the steel industry." The position really did not matter that much because by this time Jimmy Lomax had found his true vocation.

Every year, he put on the red Santa suit. Every year, there were more sick and needy children to attend to. And every year, as word of his activity spread, Jimmy collected more money and gifts to distribute.

By 1980, he was delivering more than $50,000 worth of gifts to more than 3000 people. Eventually, he was collecting more than a quarter-million dollars in donations. Much of the money came from others, but Jimmy regularly added some of his personal savings. He also took his annual vacation in the weeks leading up to Christmas so he would have time to distribute gifts to sick children, physically and mentally handicapped youngsters, and the elderly.

Operation Santa Claus became a registered charity, well known throughout the city of Hamilton. Preparing for the Christmas distribution of gifts was a year-round effort. It included a summertime garage sale, with donated items being sold to raise money for Christmas. Closer to the holiday, a Christmas gift shower was held. Anyone could attend the party, providing they brought along something to donate to Hamilton's needy and a can of food for the Hamilton food bank.

When he started out, Jimmy Lomax operated pretty much alone. Over the years, a corps of regular volunteers came to his assistance. One of the busiest was his wife Susan, a school friend and neighbour who knew Jimmy was already deeply involved in his Christmas work when they started dating. Before they were married, he made it clear that, at Christmastime, his charity work took precedence over everything. So Susan became almost as deeply involved as her husband, packaging gifts, organizing his schedule, soliciting donations, and writing thank-you notes.

The couple had one child, Ryan, born a short time before Christmas 1972. As soon as he was able, Ryan starting helping out at Christmas. For several years, he marched side by side with his father in the annual Santa Claus parade.

By the early 1980s, Jimmy Lomax was a Hamilton institution. His work brought him numerous honours. He was named Hamilton Citizen of the Year in 1981. He also received the Ontario Medal for Good Citizenship and was named to the Order of Canada. He was so well known he could not even go out drinking with a friend. In bars, people recognized him and insisted on giving him something for Operation Santa Claus.

It was difficult to mistake Jimmy Lomax for anyone else. Like Santa, he was a very large man who weighed more than 300 pounds at one point. Most years, he did not need any padding for his Santa suit. Getting the requisite long white hair and beard was a little more difficult. Some years, Jimmy grew his beard and hair and bleached them. He used correction fluid to colour his eyelashes white because it was the only thing that didn't run when he cried.

And he cried frequently. An emotional man, he was often moved to tears when encountering sick children, the handicapped, or the elderly. Usually he controlled himself by leaving the room for a few moments to regain his composure. It hurt him to see suffering, but he faced it because he understood the effect Santa has on people.

At one hospital, he brought presents to a three-year-old boy who had burns on his legs, arms, and face. At first, the child wasn't sure how to react to the big man in the red suit. Santa laughed and jingled the sleigh bells on his wrists. He sang Christmas carols to the boy and handed him several gifts. The boy was quiet, hesitant. Then Santa went down the hall to make another visit. On his way, he encountered an elderly woman sitting in a wheelchair. She was staring vacantly, but when he stopped and talked to her she smiled in recognition. Meanwhile, the little boy, with the help of his physiotherapist, had followed Santa down the corridor.

Today, Jimmy Lomax has dozens more stories about the reaction of patients to Santa's visits. One old man, bedridden for weeks, got up and danced. Jimmy frequently shares the stories with reporters, along with various opinions, some of which are unpopular. His outspokenness has offended some people, and there have been accusations of glory seeking. But, after more than 40 years of playing Santa Claus, it seems evident that Jimmy Lomax is deeply dedicated to his chosen work. "Christmas is my whole life," he once told a reporter. "I live for it from year to year."

Personal problems have not stopped him from keeping his promise to be Santa Claus. He has suffered heart attacks, serious illnesses, and has undergone hip surgery. When his father died suddenly a couple of days before the annual fundraising garage sale, Jimmy decided it should go on as usual.

Most heart wrenching of all was the loss of his only son. Ryan was diagnosed with a rare form of lung cancer while in his early teens. Everyone rallied behind the Lomax family, praying for the boy's recovery, sending cards and gifts. Although Ryan improved briefly, he died in May 1987. There was not much Christmas joy in the Lomax household that year, but Operation Santa Claus went ahead anyway. Sadly, there was more heartbreak ahead. On the anniversary of his son's death, Jimmy got drunk and decided to commit suicide by driving into a bridge abutment. He hit another car instead, sending several people to the hospital, and was later convicted of drunk driving. Still, in view of his charitable work and the tragic loss of his son, many people forgave him.

The degree of respect for Jimmy and his work was further demonstrated in 1992. For several years, Operation Santa Claus raised funds with a one-day drive at the Stelco plant.

But that year, the union asked that the drive be postponed. A day earlier, the company had announced that 800 jobs would be cut. Many of the workers were facing an uncertain future and the prospect of a Christmas without any income. Jimmy went ahead with the drive anyway, fully expecting to get less money than in the previous year. Instead, the steelworkers donated $9000, considerably more than the year before.

In recent years, Jimmy's health has deteriorated. But Operation Santa continues, proof that one inspired, determined man can spread the Christmas spirit through an entire city and beyond.

Selected Bibliography

So many newspapers, magazines, books and web sites have been consulted in preparing this manuscript that it would be impossible to list them all. However, readers interested in learning more about Christmas in Ontario, Canada or world-wide might consult the following:

Christmas in Upper Canada and Canada West: Customs and Practices (typescript). The Ted Brown Room, Niagara South Board of Education, St. Johns Outdoor Studies Centre, c. 1976. Located at Niagara Falls Public Library.

Coffin, Tristram Potter. *The Book of Christmas Folklore.* New York: Seabury Press, 1973

Crean, Patrick, editor. *The Fitzhenry & Whiteside Fireside Book of Canadian Christmas.* Toronto: Fitzhenry & Whiteside, 1986.

Knowles, Kathleen M. *To Honour the Holiday: Canadian Christmases Past.* St. John's: Creative Publishers, 1988.

Acknowledgements

Quotations used in this book have been drawn from dozens of sources, including the following books: The *Canadian Settlers Guide* by Catharine Parr Traill, *Sketches of Upper Canada* by John Howison, *River of Lights* by Cheryl Bauslaugh, *Lady Aberdeen's Diary*, *Much To Be Done* by Frances Hoffman and Ryan Taylor, *Canadian Scenery Illustrated* by N.P. Willis, *Letters from Muskoka* by an Emigrant Lady and *I Remember the One-Room School* by Mildred Fair. Newspapers and magazines from which quotations were taken include: *Brantford Expositor*, *Border Cities Star*, *Canadian Business*, *Canadian Press*, *Daily British Whig* (Kingston), *Daily Whig Standard* (Kingston), *Dryden Observer*, the *Globe and Mail*, *Hamilton Spectator*, *London Free Press*, *Maclean's Magazine*, *National Post*, *Niagara Mail*, *The Sault Evening Star*, *Toronto Star*, *Toronto Telegram*, *Toronto Evening Times*, and *Saturday Night*.

Thanks go to Andrew Porteus, manager of adult reference and information services at Niagara Falls Public Library for directing me to an invaluable resource; to Dino Fazio, general manager of Niagara Falls Winter Festival of Lights; to Laurie Papineau; to Joanne Pettes; and to Sally Szuster, publicity manager for the National Ballet of Canada. I am also grateful for access to the collections of Hamilton Public

Library, Mills Memorial Library at McMaster University and Niagara Falls Public Library, as well as for two excellent on-line resources, Early Canadiana Online and Paper of Record.

Finally, thanks go to my editors, Jill Foran and Gayl Veinotte, whose suggestions have vastly improved this book.

Photo Credits

Cover: © Richard De Wolfe. National Archives of Canada: pages 20 (Charles W. Mathers / PA-026903), 25 (Ken Bell / PA-189262), 47 (Ellen H. Clapsaddle / C-042966), 74 (John Boyd / PA-071301).

Cover image provided courtesy of
Richard De Wolfe Fine Art
280 Mud Lake Road N
Odessa, Ontario, Canada K0H 2H0
Phone: (615) 386-7677 Fax: (613) 386-7681
Email: rdewolfe1@home.com
Web Site: www.richarddewolfe.com

About the Author

Cheryl MacDonald has been writing about Canadian history for nearly 30 years. A long-time resident of Nanticoke, she is a full-time writer and historian whose weekly history column appears in the *Simcoe Times-Reformer*. Her historical articles have appeared in *The Beaver, Maclean's*, the *Hamilton Spectator* and *The Old Farmer's Almanac*. Cheryl has also written more than a dozen books on Canadian and Ontario history, including Amazing Stories titles *Niagara Daredevils* and *Great Canadian Love Stories*. She is currently completing a master's degree in history at McMaster University, Hamilton.

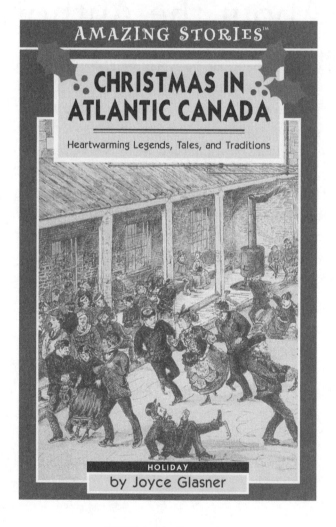

AMAZING STORIES™

:·CHRISTMAS IN·:
ATLANTIC CANADA

Heartwarming Legends, Tales, and Traditions

HOLIDAY
by Joyce Glasner

ISBN 1-55153-781-8

AMAZING STORIES™

CHRISTMAS IN QUEBEC

Heartwarming Legends, Tales, and Traditions

HOLIDAY

by Megan Durnford

ISBN 1-55153-784-2

OTHER AMAZING STORIES

ISBN	Title	Author
1-55153-943-8	Black Donnellys	Nate Hendley
1-55153-947-0	Canada's Rumrunners	Art Montague
1-55153-966-7	Canadian Spies	Tom Douglas
1-55153-795-8	D-Day	Tom Douglas
1-55153-982-9	Dinosaur Hunters	Lisa Murphy-Lamb
1-55153-970-5	Early Voyageurs	Marie Savage
1-55153-968-3	Edwin Alonzo Boyd	Nate Hendley
1-55153-996-9	Emily Carr	Cat Klerks
1-55153-973-X	Great Canadian Love Stories	Cheryl MacDonald
1-55153-946-2	Great Dog Stories	Roxanne Snopek
1-55153-942-X	The Halifax Explosion	Joyce Glasner
1-55153-958-6	Hudson's Bay Company Adventures	Elle Andra-Warner
1-55153-969-1	Klondike Joe Boyle	Stan Sauerwein
1-55153-980-2	Legendary Show Jumpers	Debbie G-Arsenault
1-55153-979-9	Ma Murray	Stan Sauerwein
1-55153-964-0	Marilyn Bell	Patrick Tivy
1-55153-953-5	Moe Norman	Stan Sauerwein
1-55153-962-4	Niagara Daredevils	Cheryl MacDonald
1-55153-945-4	Pierre Elliott Trudeau	Stan Sauerwein
1-55153-981-0	Rattenbury	Stan Sauerwein
1-55153-991-8	Rebel Women	Linda Kupecek
1-55153-956-X	Robert Service	Elle Andra-Warner
1-55153-952-7	Strange Events	Johanna Bertin
1-55153-954-3	Snowmobile Adventures	Linda Aksomitis
1-55153-950-0	Tom Thomson	Jim Poling Sr.
1-55153-976-4	Trailblazing Sports Heroes	Joan Dixon
1-55153-977-2	Unsung Heroes of the RCAF	Cynthia J. Faryon
1-55153-959-4	A War Bride's Story	Cynthia Faryon
1-55153-948-9	The War of 1812 Against the States	Jennifer Crump

These titles are available wherever you buy books. If you have trouble finding the book you want, call the Altitude order desk at 1-800-957-6888, e-mail your request to: orderdesk@altitudepublishing.com or visit our Web site at www.amazingstories.ca

New AMAZING STORIES titles are published every month.